MISSING, BELIEVED KILLED

MISSING, BELIEVED KILLED

THE REMARKABLE STORY OF A
JAPANESE POW CAMP SURVIVOR

John Baxter

First published in Great Britain 2010
by Aurum Press Ltd
7 Greenland Street
London NW1 0ND
www.aurumpress.co.uk

A catalogue record for this book is available
from the British Library

ISBN 978 1 84513 538 6

Typeset in Bell by David Fletcher Welch
Plate section designed by David Fletcher Welch
Printed in the UK by MPG Books, Bodmin, Cornwall

CONTENTS

Foreword   ix

Acknowledgements   xi

Abbreviations   xiii

Chapter 1   1
Training, Blitz and Bomb Disposal

Chapter 2   13
Off Abroad

Chapter 3   25
Action In Java

Chapter 4   39
In the Bag

Chapter 5   45
Promises, Promises!

Chapter 6   63
Bogor 'Hospital'

Chapter 7   75
The PoW War Effort

Chapter 8   93
Out and About

Chapter 9   99
Bicycle Camp

Chapter 10   107
Boie Glodok and Tjimahi

Chapter 11   119
Singapore and Points East

Chapter 12   131
Japan

Chapter 13   137
The Mines

Chapter 14   145
The Shaft

Chapter 15   151
Spanners in the Works

Chapter 16   167
Beginning of the End

Chapter 17   179
PoWs in Occupation

Chapter 18   189
Starting Homewards

Chapter 19   201
Flight to the Philippines

Chapter 20   209
Pacific Passage

Chapter 21   217
Canada, Queen Mary and Home

Postscript   223

APPENDIXES

1   Translation of speech by the new Commandant of   227
     Tandjong Priok Camp in 1942

2   Transcript of document issued at Tandjong   229
     Priok in 1942 for prisoners to write to loved ones

3   Names and places of origin at time of capture   231
     of Services personnel in the PoW camp at
     Tandjong Priok

4   Medical report on 8 Camp by PoW Medical 1.9.45   237

5   Average weights of British personnel, No. 8.   247
     PoW Camp, Fukuoka

6   Report on working conditions – 8 Camp,   249
     Fukuoka, Japan, 1.9.45

7   Red Cross benefits received between   257
     13.10.43 and 28.8.45

8   Translation of speech by the Japanese Colonel   261
     at No. 11 Camp, Fukuoka, on 20.8.45

9   Locations visited by the author from leaving   263
     the UK in 1941

10   Extract from document presented in evidence to   265
     the War Crimes Trials showing steps Japanese
     camp commandants were expected to take to rid
     themselves of PoWs

FOREWORD

The hammering woke me with a start.

When I'd arrived in the 'hospital', this small room had had twelve more occupants, lying on boards laid on the tiled floor. When one died there was hammering in the room next door, as they made his coffin. I arrived twelve days ago; now, after twelve nights of hammering, I was the last one left – and they were hammering again! What did that mean for my own chance of surviving to the following day?

———

That was in Java in 1942, nearly seventy years ago, and I'm still here writing about it. I survived! Indeed my life was saved twice over: that brush with death prevented me being drafted out with other REME PoWs to Borneo, where most of them perished in the hell-hole of Kuching Camp. Also, when a convoy was taking us to Japan to work in the Kyushu coal mines, if the ship alongside us had not turned into the track of the torpedo heading for the *Ussuri Maru*, I would have died then too. And then, to cap it all, there was the Nagasaki bomb, dropped some 40 miles away from the mines, whose vast mushroom cloud I saw rising hundreds of feet into the sky, and whose blast of heat ignited the coal dust covering prisoners as they emerged from the mine entrance.

That is one of the most striking things about my involuntary circumnavigation of the wartime world... how many occasions there were when I survived but so easily might not have.

This is an account of one serviceman's experiences in World War II, from Paddington Station to Papworth Hospital via Java, Japan and San Francisco. They included three years as a prisoner of the Japanese until VJ Day (15 August 1945). No heroics are intended – merely a chronicle of events as they happened, supported by fragments of a wartime diary, information gleaned from former comrades, and above all, a long memory.

The story is authentic and, if nothing else, illustrates the futility of war. After intensive military and engineering training I, like many thousands of others, was shipped out to foreign fields, only, after a short-lived campaign, to find all this preparation brought to nothing. The hard-earned expertise was wasted and all the accompanying technical impedimenta had to be destroyed by our own men before it could be used. After that, life had to be conducted in an alien climate and an alien culture and became a matter of survival, surreptitious sabotage and holding on to the greatest survival aid of all: a (well-concealed) sense of humour.

John Baxter, 2010

ACKNOWLEDGEMENTS

I am indebted to the following people who helped make this book possible:

The late Peter Williams (former Captain, 48th LAA Regt) for permission to reprint copies of his 1945 Report to the War Crimes Commission.

The late Eddie Hawkins, former Secretary to the Cardiff Branch of the Far East Prisoners of War (FEPOW) Association, for providing excerpts from monthly newsletters and photographs.

Last, but certainly not least, I am grateful to all members of my family and friends for the many hours spent in typing, word-processing, photocopying and proof-reading in order to make this book possible.

ABBREVIATIONS

ATS — Auxiliary Territorial Service

CO — Commanding Officer

COFEPOW — Children and Families of Far East Prisoners of War

cwt — Hundredweight

DDT — Dichlorodiphenyl-trichloroethane (a pesticide)

DZ — Drop zone – the area into which men or supplies are parachuted from an aircraft

ENSA — Entertainments National Service Association

FEPOW — Far East Prisoner of War

GI — Government Issue (in United States – hence American soldier)

HAA — Heavy ack ack

LAA — Light ack ack

MI — Medical inspection

MO — Medical orderly

NAAFI — Navy, Army & Air Force Institute

NCOs — Non-Commissioned Officers

PoW — Prisoner of war

PX — Post Exchange – the US name for canteens

RAF — Royal Air Force

RAMC — Royal Army Medical Corps

RASC — Royal Army Service Corps

RE — Royal Engineers

REME — Royal Electrical & Mechanical Engineers

VJ — Victory over Japan

CHAPTER 1
Training, Blitz and Bomb Disposal

On a cold March morning in 1941 a motley crowd of recruits assembled at Paddington Station. They were mainly in the 38–41 age group, but some were technicians recalled after previous deferment. I was one of these, having first registered before the war in March 1939 under the Militia Training Act, which required all men between 20 and 21 to serve for six months and then spend 3½ years in the reserve. Because my occupation was in the 'reserved' category (I was a plumbing and heating engineer), my call-up had been twice deferred, but now a severe shortage of all types of engineers meant the youngest reserved technicians were being called to the colours to replace men lost at Dunkirk and in the Middle East. I was now one of 1,500 conscripts, mostly older than me, on draft to a military training centre 'somewhere in Wales'.

After an hour's delay, we boarded a train made up of nondescript, careworn coaches to start the first of the many long and frustrating journeys that were a feature of wartime troop movements. At that time rail travel was best avoided, since it involved all the hazards of black-outs and air raids, not to mention ancient rolling stock, no station destination boards, shortage of water in the toilets (if any) and limited catering facilities in station buffets.

Most of my fellow travellers had brought sandwiches and the odd thermos flask of tea or coffee, or a bottle of beer. This was just as well, because it was 14½ hours before we finally ended up after dark at Pembroke Dock in Carmarthenshire. (After a heavy air raid while we were in a siding at Cardiff station, we had been diverted around the Welsh valleys to avoid priority rail traffic, adding another couple of hours to our trip.) It was about three-quarters of a mile from Pembroke station to the old barracks on the hill above the town, and we shuffled off through the darkened streets guided by a solitary NCO with a dim torch who told us, 'Keep up and no straggling! There's a hot meal ready for you up at the camp'. We found that, like many Army promises, this one was rather inexact. It takes time to process 1,500 men in any organisation, and, after being laboriously checked in by half a dozen orderly room clerks, it was at least an hour before we finally received the most important part of our army kit – a knife, fork and spoon – and were directed to the garrison mess hall.

Our first army meal of beef steak, potatoes and beans did reassure us that service life was not all bad and compensated a little for our earlier frustrations. Afterwards we were told to go off in groups to occupy our billets: some Victorian married quarters, complete with cast-iron kitchen stoves. The rooms were quite spartan, with curtains or floor coverings and only World War I iron army beds, on which were neatly piled three coarse blankets and three 3ft × 2ft 'biscuit' type hard mattresses. If one was lucky enough to be in the kitchen area, some level of heat could be expected, but there was no semblance of warmth anywhere. Even the comfort of the kitchen occupants proved short-lived, as the weekly ration of half a hundredweight of coal petered out by midweek, despite the most miserly stoking. That didn't worry us on our first night in barracks, though; we were too tired to light fires, and midnight found us making the most of our hard and unfamiliar army beds. Those used to more comfortable surroundings spent the rest of the night in pretty fitful sleep, accompanied by a chorus of snores from their new bedfellows.

At the unearthly hour of 5.30 a.m. the strident notes of a bugle introduced us to 'Reveille', and were accompanied by the raucous voice of a drill-sergeant requesting us to appear:

'Outside! At the double! In vests, shorts, and gym shoes!'

It was quite dark outside and must have been near freezing, but we were not allowed to dwell on it. After a short session of 'running on the spot' and an attempt to muster us in columns of four, the whole company of coughing, wheezing, teeth-chattering recruits was led off at a steady trot through the barrack gates. Following an NCO gym instructor, we 'trotted' through the deserted streets of Pembroke into open country, making a large circuit that finally brought us back to camp. This was our introduction to a daily routine, a three-mile jog before breakfast, 'to get rid of the cobwebs' as one old sweat put it. As a keen cyclist and walker, I was pretty fit, and this did not worry me unduly, but I felt sorry for some of the older men whose civilian jobs had not conditioned them to such physical rigours. The stragglers would inevitably be arriving back for breakfast to face cold porridge and whatever was left of a cooked meal well after their predecessors had eaten their fill.

Straight after this we plunged into a hectic programme of training sessions ranging from foot and arms drill, weapon training, assault courses and unarmed combat to the more theoretical pursuits of lectures, intelligence tests and camouflage techniques. And we were not allowed to get bored in the evenings: everyone was detailed on time-consuming activities like guard duty, fire piquet, air raid precautions or kitchen fatigue. The last one was a firm favourite; it ensured that one was usually in the warm cookhouse, and it often resulted in 'perks' in the shape of extra food!

I blotted my copy book for the first time in my army career whilst on kitchen duty. I and another recruit were carrying coal in a twin-handled tin bath from an outside dump to the cookhouse boiler. En route we encountered an officer, and, dutifully, we both saluted – I with my left hand, as my right arm was grasping the bath handle. After admonishing me for saluting wrongly, the officer awarded me another seven day's kitchen fatigues (a blessing in disguise – it saved me from a cold main-gate guard duty!).

No one was allowed outside the camp in the evenings until it we had attained a 'soldierly appearance', which apparently took at least two weeks training. During the few hours between other duties that we could call free time, our only source of entertainment was the camp NAAFI, which boasted a battered wartime utility radio and an equally nondescript piano of suspect vintage. If we were not listening to the news, or Tommy Handley in *ITMA*, someone sufficiently primed with the warm beer on sale would 'tinkle the ivories', and we would have a sing-song. Alternative liquid refreshment was standard NAAFI-grade tea (wherever one was posted, at home or abroad, its unique quality and taste never varied). The same could be said of the slab cake purveyed at all NAAFIs, which looked and tasted like sawdust and was always cut in three-inch squares exactly three-quarters of an inch thick.

An ENSA concert party visited us during our training, but, their dubious fame having preceded them, on the first night the auditorium was empty except for one row of embarrassed officers and senior NCO's. The next evening all personnel in camp not on other duties were paraded and marched into the concert hall as 'volunteers' to enjoy the extravaganza. Two elderly gentlemen with violin and cello, and an equally ancient lady on piano, regaled us with an hour's chamber music that was not altogether improved by sundry missing notes on the piano and the inability of the older gentleman to keep pace with the pianist!

Meanwhile our intensive training continued apace, and, after passing small-arms tests on the firing range, we filled in with first-aid courses, water-purification instruction, fire-fighting and route marching in full kit. Air raids were minimal compared to my home in London, where nightly bombing was the norm. However, German mine-laying aircraft visited the offshore concentrations of shipping, where convoys assembled before moving into the Atlantic. No bombs fell on the town or its surroundings while we were training but there were enough alerts to keep us on our toes, manning the local defences and fire-fighting appliances. The Army Fire Brigade was in its infancy in March 1941, and Pembroke Dock had a contingent consisting of two Leyland fire tenders and two trailer pumps with one officer and 24 men and NCOs.

When our Company Sergeant Major asked for anyone with any knowledge of pumps, I naively stepped forward, thinking that, given my pre-war occupation as a plumber, my expertise might be required on the camp heating installation. Not so! I now discovered why I had been advised never to volunteer for anything: I was posted to one of the trailer pump teams. The Army Fire Brigade detachment had been sent to augment the local Auxiliary Fire Service (AFS), whose responsibility was the huge fuel storage tanks at Pembroke Dock. Hence, during one air raid alert I was on duty with two others at a trailer pump parked inside the barracks perimeter. Our Army fire officer had advised us that this was a superficial exercise, as the pump was awaiting repairs to a broken big end, and so was out of action. But during the 'stand-to' all the outposts around the barracks were favoured by a visit from a rather pompous Orderly Officer. He felt the radiator of our trailer pump, found it stone cold and became very officious.

'Don't you know that this must be started up in readiness at every alert?' he shouted.

'Its big end has gone sir!'

'I don't care what's gone. You know what Standing Orders say. Start it up!'

Without further argument, we did so, and the pump motor fired with an almighty clatter. 'Standing Orders' required a quarter of an hour's warm up, it seemed, and the officer stolidly listened to a variety of expensive noises from the labouring engine. After fifteen minutes he checked his watch and ordered us to switch off.

'Don't let it occur again, or you will all be on a charge,' he said, stalking off.

When we finished our initial training in April, the course broke up into various parties for posting to units all over Britain. At the same time, higher authority decided the Army Fire Brigade would be more use elsewhere. So I found myself accompanying a draft of sixty recruits, mostly technicians, and the Fire Brigade unit en route to London. This time we went by road in a convoy of two single-decker coaches, followed by the two fire engines and their trailers. (Ironically, the night after we left, Pembroke Dock suffered its heaviest raid of the war. Several parachute mines, incendiaries and large bombs fell on the oil installations, and a massive conflagration required back-up fire appliances from all over South Wales and burned fiercely for three weeks!)

Meanwhile, our little convoy arrived in London at the height of an air raid, and once again we were forced to detour several times before we reached our destination – Charing Cross Station. Our sixty recruits had been meant to de-bus and take a waiting train to Woolwich Military Depot, but shortly before we arrived the train had taken a direct hit, spreading debris across all the tracks and preventing anything entering or leaving the station. Simultaneously a heavy incendiary raid had set to several large buildings in the vicinity alight, and we found our two coaches encircled by blazing fires and several Auxiliary Fire Service (AFS) appliances endeavouring to extinguish them. Our two fire tenders swiftly went into operation to help pump water from the Thames to supplement the hard-pressed street hydrants.

When there was a break in the waves of aircraft overhead, the Railway Transport officer told us to proceed to Woolwich by road, as rail repairs would not be possible until morning. For the next hour we drove on, now through the debris-laden streets of south London, running the gauntlet of further fires, collapsing buildings and the hazards of our own shrapnel, which rained down almost continuously as the raiders returned. We finally de-bussed in the blacked-out confines of Cambridge Barracks, Woolwich, and settled down on the hard floor of the main lecture hall to grab what sleep we could before another phase of our army service began in the morning. No such luxury as iron beds for us that night!

Woolwich, a large garrison area in the south-eastern suburbs of London, consisted of several large barracks, the Royal Military Academy and a mass of army workshops known as the Repository. It was to the last that most tradesmen were drafted, and we found ourselves billeted in some married quarters vacated by the original occupants. Then we then settled down to more intensive technical training. Shortly after I arrived I was lucky enough to meet a peacetime acquaintance who had trained me in welding techniques and was now a Staff Sergeant instructor. Through his recommendation I swiftly found myself elevated to the rank of corporal and proceeded to take over the two-week courses in welding repairs. These were organised to train fitters, mechanics and sheet-metal workers in first-aid repairs to a range of army equipment encompassing all forms of transport, armaments and other military hardware.

This posting lasted six months and, apart from the privileges enjoyed by an NCO, it also brought the advantage of close proximity of home – a mere twenty-five miles away – and the chance to sample home comforts once in a while. But life in Woolwich was no picnic; we suffered over 380 air raids in the six months I was stationed there, and I do not recall having one full night's sleep during that period. Staff shortages meant that all workshop personnel, including the hapless trainees, were expected, indeed detailed, to take part in night duty of some sort on five nights out of seven. This could be main-gate guard, fire piquet, telephone orderly, first-aid stretcher-bearer, rescue and demolition, anti-paratrooper patrol or anything else the sergeant major could think of. And as raids started at dusk and rarely ended before dawn, it was usually a hectic night for everyone. The surrounding anti-aircraft batteries kept me awake even if the bombs didn't.

In the area around Woolwich Arsenal alone, there were several 16-gun batteries of 3.7mm anti-aircraft guns, together with dozens of Bofors and a 64-tube rocket battery; and on Plumstead Marshes to the south a battery of huge 9.2mm guns added to the general din. Anyone out in the open during raids stood a fair chance of being injured by the rain of falling shrapnel from our own anti-aircraft shells. On the morning after, it was not uncommon to recover several wheelbarrows full of jagged pieces of metal from the roads and parade ground or the workshop area alone. On the few occasions that I was able to get a pass home, my time was usually spent dozing, the result of exhaustion and lack of sleep.

After several months of these heavy raids, it became difficult to maintain continuity in the workshop training programmes, and it was decided to move lock, stock and barrel to a safer area. All machinery and equipment was duly crated up and loaded for despatch to the new location at Donnington Park, near Derby. I was packed ready for departure like everyone else when I received last-minute instructions to unpack my welding equipment and stand by for transfer elsewhere.

—◦—

After sitting alone in the deserted workshops for about an hour, I was interested to see a bomb disposal truck reversing in.

'Sorry lads,' I said. 'The workshops are closed, no further repairs are being carried out here.'

'Jump in,' said the driver. 'It's you I've come for!'

I discovered that my oxyacetylene cutting kit was the only one in the immediate area, and my services were urgently required to clear some tangled steelwork where a delayed-action bomb rested. I didn't have much time to consider the consequences, but this first encounter with a live bomb was a jittery experience. One never knew whether the heavy steel sections being cut would fall and set off the contrivance below, and the showers of sparks from the oxyacetylene burner was a further hazard, particularly when there were fractured oil pipes or gas mains nearby. However, an hour's sweaty work soon cleared the way for the digging gang, and I retired to a safe distance while the bomb was carefully exposed and finally defused by the accompanying officer.

This was the start of a brief spell with the area bomb-disposal group, which had been sadly depleted during the past months. The section I was attached to numbered 24 men in all with one officer. All senior NCOs had been killed, and I found myself, a corporal, senior to two lance corporals who were both Royal Engineers. The rest of the rank and file were half Royal Engineers and half conscientious objectors, from the Pioneer Corps, who had volunteered to undertake the hazardous 'non-combatant' task of digging out bombs. No special danger money was awarded to bomb-disposal squads; the only concession was payment of a full tradesman's pay to RE personnel and one shilling a day ration money in lieu of a midday meal, as most units were away from their billets during the day. Every type of fiendish device was used by the Germans to make life difficult for the bomb-disposal parties, and in the short time I was with them we encountered acoustic and magnetic mines and bombs, and several aerial mines up to 15 feet long and 18 inches in diameter. Clearing away a delayed-action bomb needed extreme care, as the Germans often secured these by a cable or chain to two or more other bombs that might be covered in the surrounding debris. On one occasion, we had to help cut up a complete double-decker tramcar, which had fallen into a 30-foot crater at Charlton.

The eeriest job I can remember was searching for five delayed-action bombs inside a gas-holder at Beckton Gas Works. Fortunately the gas-holder was empty when it was hit, but the major difficulty was the foul water in the base which necessitated a probing exercise in a makeshift punt, once pumps finally reduced the water level and exposed the points of entry of the bombs. We eventually retrieved what we thought were all the bombs that had dropped into that particular gas-holder. We had counted five large holes in its cover, but we had not realised that one 1,000lb bomb must have come through a hole made by a previous bomb. That sixth bomb stayed undetected for 45 years, until Friday 21 November 1986 when maintenance engineers from the Gas Board came across a leak in the gas-holder. The muck and foul-smelling rubbish at the bottom of the gas-holder was still there, because divers had to be called for, and an ex-Marine civilian diver discovered what he thought felt like a bomb.

The modern equivalent of our bomb-disposal squad was hurriedly called in, consisting of Major Robbie Hall and Sapper Paul Wright. They soon confirmed that it was indeed a bomb and set about uncovering and identifying it. Given that the bomb had lain there for so long, both the fuse and the explosive were liable to be unpredictably treacherous. This meant that houses had to be evacuated for up to three-quarters of a mile around, and it took these two brave men 21 hours cooped up inside the gas holder to defuse the bomb. For this, both were rightly awarded the Queen's Gallantry Medal in February 1988.[*]

For our group of men there were few awards – such tasks were everyday duties, and many never lived to be presented with an award anyway. Originally, the Bomb Disposal Squad contingent had been three hundred strong, but after six months of casualties our section of 24 was all that remained. Sadly, within a week of my joining the unit a further 12 men were killed or seriously wounded when a 1,000lb delayed-action bomb exploded as they were preparing to deal with it. It was therefore with great relief that I received orders to report back to Woolwich for posting to a mobile workshop unit in the Nottingham area, well away from such dangers.

[*] An account of this incident was published in the April 1988 edition of *the Reader's Digest.*

CHAPTER 2
Off Abroad

Two days and one railway warrant from St Pancras Station later I found myself in the drill hall at Carlton in Nottingham, where I learned:

    (a) that I was to be attached to the 7th Armoured Division, and

    (b) that my first seven days' leave was due.

I wasted no time in collecting my leave documents and returned to London post haste for a welcome break from army routine at my parents' home in Ealing!

A week later I returned to Nottingham to discover that the 7th Armoured Division had left for the Middle East without me, and I was now the sole occupant of a deserted Gospel Hall, formerly one of their outlying billets. It was a bit spooky sleeping in this vast building at night, but by day there was no one around to order me about! Mealtimes were a simple matter of joining the queue at the nearby drill hall. However, like all good things in the Army, this situation ended abruptly: a suspicious sergeant major noticed one NCO too many on the ration strength. Accordingly, I was detailed in charge of, first, the main-gate guard and, secondly, defaulters – whose main tasks seemed to be latrine-clearing and sweeping non-existent dust from the immaculate floors of the drill hall.

As a mobilisation centre, Carlton was involved in making up deficiencies in men and materials for most outgoing overseas drafts. The surrounding countryside abounded in equipment stores and vast vehicle parks, and an ever-changing stream of personnel passed through the depot before being allocated for service abroad. There were numerous courses to occupy the mind in the days or weeks spent awaiting a posting, and time passed quickly and pleasantly compared to London, where life was infinitely more hazardous. All NCOs were sent on a commando-style toughening-up course under canvas in Bulwell Park. Unfortunately it rained for most of the two weeks, which, coupled with the hazing we received from the Grenadier Guards instructors, made our stay unforgettable. The discipline and stamina acquired in surviving that ordeal were not appreciated at the time, but the lessons learned were to prove absolutely invaluable later.

Everyone destined for a mobile workshop unit was expected to have driving experience, and I prepared for anticipated instruction by buying a 'Learn to Drive' manual, and by the time orders for my training came through I had absorbed most of the important details. I arrived at the army driving instruction centre and was mistakenly directed to a group of trainees awaiting their final test. When my turn came to take the wheel of the truck I did so quite happily, armed with my do-it-yourself-book knowledge, and started off successfully, bowling merrily along the main road, the instructor by my side and half a dozen unsuspecting trainee drivers in the back. Gear-changing and double declutching was going according to the book, and so far no comment from the instructor. At one point in a narrow road we met a long convoy of large ambulances driven by women ATS. Still assuming that the instructor knew that I was a novice, I felt that now was the time for some friendly advice, but no, he was still gazing steadfastly ahead and saying nothing. More by luck than judgement I negotiated the gaps between the oncoming vehicles without so much as scraping the paintwork, and it was with some relief that we finally passed through and the instructor called a halt.

'OK,' he said: 'Reverse into that narrow lane.'

This I did, bumping over the kerb in the process.

'You'll not pass your test like that!' he rebuked me.

'Hold on a minute,' I protested, 'I haven't done so bad so far, considering it's my first time behind the wheel.'

The instructor went a bit pale.

'Are you telling me I've let you drive us all the way from Nottingham and you haven't had one lesson?'

'Yes.'

The obviously shaken NCO immediately took the wheel and drove the truck back to base. The rest of my instruction passed off satisfactorily – although I noticed that a different instructor completed my course!

After this course I received my final posting: to the headquarters company of a mobile workshop unit attached to a Radar and Anti-Aircraft regiment. This was situated at a large country house in its own grounds on the outskirts of Nottingham, where the Sergeant Major appointed me NCO in charge of motorcycles. My protest that I knew nothing about motorcycles fell on deaf ears; I was a spare corporal and must be found a job, and this one was nobody's pigeon. The unit was just forming and no despatch riders had so far joined the strength, although several new machines had arrived. My first task was to fit sand filters to all the carburettors, as we were apparently destined for the desert. Then I set out to learn how to ride these monsters solely by trial and error – which I did over the next fortnight at the cost of a few bruises, bent foot-rests and encounters with local hedges. Over the next few weeks, the unit grew to operational strength with an influx of tradesmen ranging from instrument mechanics and armourers to driver/mechanics, fitters and welders.

As an independent mobile workshop company, we were expected to be able to repair and service all instruments from wrist-watches to large gunnery predictors, all vehicles from motorcycles to 55-ton tanks and all armaments from ·38 revolvers to the largest field piece or anti-aircraft gun. Our full complement of men was 120, with 32 vehicles, including stores – so, to handle the range of specialist trades, everyone, including officers, had to be capable of doing two or more jobs as well as being able to drive. Furthermore, we were responsible for our own defence, cooking and other mundane occupations necessary to keep an independent unit functioning. To gain working-up experience we were attached to several other units and travelled from one area to another, living in our trucks and subsisting on ration packs except on the rare occasions when we stopped overnight at military bases (where we caught up on our mail, usually a week late).

Much of our work consisted of erecting radar installations near prime target areas. The early radar units were rather primitive and consisted of a control cabin with antennae, sited in the centre of a suitably large field and surrounded by a horizontal mat of wire mesh about 100 yards square, which acted as a receiving aerial. These mats were usually made of rabbit wire stretched taut over a forest of angle-iron supports driven into the ground and levelled regardless of the contours of the field below. Unfortunately these trampoline-like structures would glisten with dew in the moonlight and make a tempting target for enemy aircraft, even though many of them had little idea that what they had hit was a radar installation. It was particularly soul-destroying and frustrating to have to repair these installations after bombs had turned them into a tangled mass of twisted angle and wire, particularly as it they had to be restored to full operation as quickly as possible.

After some months on mobile operations in the Midlands, we were ordered to join an overseas draft and moved to Liverpool to spend the few weeks before departure preparing for embarkation. Those due for leave departed shortly after we got there, myself included, while the rest crated up equipment not wanted on the voyage and camouflaged vehicles for desert warfare. After my leave I returned to Liverpool at the height of an air raid to an almost empty barracks: all available men and spare vehicles had been rushed to the docks to assist in the disembarkation and rapid dispersal of a large convoy that had arrived from Canada. It transpired that, at this crucial time, the dockers had seen fit to go on strike – which did not endear them to the troops who were feverishly carrying out their unloading operations during a heavy air raid and at considerably lower rates of pay. In spite of several casualties and some damage to equipment, by dawn several thousand Canadians and their impedimenta had safely driven away to various inland destinations, and the empty ships were ready to receive our outgoing drafts.

The dock strike (which was over pay) lasted all the following week, and despite all entreaties by the authorities, emphasising the urgency of the situation (after all, chaps, there was a war on!), the dockers remained adamant. So, to ensure that the convoy left on the prescribed date, we had to load the ships ourselves! Again this was not very well received by the troops, particularly those of us due to leave our shores to pursue the war for the benefit of the offending strikers. However, with help from the Docks Admin Officers and ships' crews we tackled the huge task of loading all the trucks, stores and other paraphernalia that accompanied the units bound overseas. Finally, all was stowed away, and the cargo ships left to form up before joining the main convoy. The hurried loading and the inexperience of many troops in securing certain items of cargo were to have consequences later, though, and for a long while the word 'dockers' could not be uttered without prompting a great deal of blue language.

The intense bombing made it impossible to complete loading all the ships, and some left overnight for the Firth of Clyde, where any vehicles still awaiting stowage and their personnel could embark under more congenial conditions. None of our heavy vehicles had been put aboard, and so they had to go by road convoy to Glasgow. This turned out to be one of the coldest journeys we had yet endured, with biting winds and sleet for the entire twelve hours the journey took at the regulation convoy speed of 30 mph. (It must be remembered that all our vehicles had been converted for desert warfare and had no heaters, only canvas doors, and the windscreens on any that had them were only half-circles of glass that hardly protected the cab occupants, who were muffled up in two layers of underclothes, greatcoats, balaclavas, mittens and gas capes.) In spite of all these clothes everyone was perishing cold, and we made more than the usual number of halts to try and brew warming tea by bleak Lancastrian roadsides. We were promised a hot meal at Carlisle, the last stop before Glasgow, but this, served at the roadside by the local RASC depot, turned out to be a small bun and a cup of lukewarm cocoa per man.

So it was a disconsolate body of drivers and their companions that finally rolled into the dockside at Gourock, Clydeside, and loud were the demands for something to satisfy the inner man; we had been travelling all night, and our last substantial meal had been at teatime in Liverpool, twelve hours before. Our requests fell on deaf ears, and, to add insult to injury, we were asked to help load some lighters with equipment belonging to someone else's unit. After an hour of this unsought labour, someone discovered a Church of Scotland canteen at the end of the docks, and everyone made a bee line for it and joined the queue. We had worked our way patiently to within a dozen places of the canteen door when stentorian voices indicated that a tender was waiting to embark our unit and take us immediately to a troopship standing out in the Firth of Clyde. Reluctantly we took our places on the tender, which proceeded out into the Firth, rolling heavily to the distress of those fortunate (or unfortunate) enough to have had a meal. Our unit was too dispirited and hungry to worry about the motion, and in any case our attention was diverted by a last-minute issue of mail – the last we were likely to get from home for a long time. In our state of depression it would have been nice to have had some comforting word from home, but the only letter I got was from the Inspector of Taxes, telling me that I still owed him £11 for the period before I was called up!

At last we reached the trooper, which proved to be the pre-war Union Castle boat, *Warwick Castle*, now in regulation grey paint with the number HMT.Z16 on her bows. We filed aboard, settled into our quarters and finally were led to the large dining deck, where a sumptuous meal of beef and potatoes was waiting. The dining staff must have sensed our needs, and for a while we felt like pre-war tourists. Later we retired, replete, and forgot our recent tribulations in deep and well earned sleep.

When we awoke, we were steaming to rendezvous with other ships of the convoy assembling off the Irish Coast. At breakfast, the radio announced that the Japanese had attacked Pearl Harbor, and both America and we were now at war with Japan. This was momentous news, but we did not feel it concerned us initially, as it had been revealed that we were part of a large force travelling to Abadan in Iran, to provide a military railway and anti-aircraft defences in that country to counter the German threat of inva-sion of the Near East.

During the morning we were initiated into boat drill and other essential duties, such as manning the defences on board (Bofors anti-aircraft guns and Bren machine-guns), operating watertight bulkhead doors, etc. These were routine tasks on convoys, but doubly important at this time, as it was the peak of the Battle of the Atlantic, and we could expect attacks at any time from both aircraft and submarines.

It was also a particularly rough time to travel: December conditions were normally the worst, and an uncomfortable passage could be expected. The seas were indeed pretty mountainous, with forty-foot waves often obscuring the other ships in the convoy. This consisted of about thirty merchant vessels escorted by several corvettes and, several miles astern, the battleship *Ramillies*. To our starboard was the troopship *Empress of Australia* carrying 3,500 men, and to port was a 5,000-ton tramp steamer *City of Pretoria*, closely followed by the 3,500-ton *Troilus*. These two ships carried our transport, the heavy trucks secured on deck with smaller vehicles below. The *Troilus* also carried as deck cargo several large railway engines and rolling stock destined for the Iran railway. The locos, converted to run on oil, had been collected from the Great Western Railway's Swindon works, along with a Royal Engineers Railway Unit from the Longmoor Military Railway in Hampshire, which were to operate them.

On the second night of our voyage, the air-raid warning sounded, and a long-range Focke Wulf *Condor* aircraft dropped several bombs and mines before being driven off by the combined anti-aircraft salvoes from the ships. During the violent evasive action most ships took during the raid, the *City of Pretoria* signalled that shifting cargo was affecting her steering. We later learned from the skeleton staff travelling with the transport that several lorries had broken loose in the hold and crashed into other vehicles and crated cargo, and the whole unmanageable mass of shifting debris had caused a list. It took three days of superhuman effort by the crew and army personnel, at considerable risk to life and limb, before the moving mass of vehicles was finally secured. This after-effect of indifferent stowage during the dock strike resulted in irreparable damage to many essential vehicles and the ruin of food and other stores by spilt oil and crushing.

Some days after this we encountered much calmer weather and, on Christmas Day 1941, we steamed into Freetown harbour in Sierra Leone to take on water and fuel. Here we learned that a U-boat which had been shadowing our convoy had been sunk by the battleship *Ramillies* travelling some miles astern. Without sea breezes to cool us, the humid temperature rose to 100°F (38°C) in the shade, and we spent what must have been for most of us our hottest Christmas ever. Of course, the cooks made no concession at all to the tropical conditions and we stoically munched through traditional roast turkey with all the trimmings followed by steaming plum pudding and hot custard! At least it was a bit better than the cocoa and bun in Carlisle!

We left Freetown late on Boxing Day for the next leg of our journey, arriving several days later at Cape Town, where all troops were allowed ashore for a five-day break from shipboard life. After the wartime austerity and blackout conditions of England, Cape Town was a paradise of lights and plenty, and the hospitality of the residents something to remember. I was fortunate in meeting an expatriate English couple who had lived in Cape Province for twenty years and now had a son in the South African army, serving in the Middle East. The husband, an emergency linesman with the Cape Colony Power Company, was provided by his employer with a bright red Pontiac, complete with siren, in which I was whisked around the sights. Our tour included a drive high up on Table Mountain at night to view the glittering panorama of Cape Town's illuminations.

All good things come to an end, sadly, and on the fifth night we slipped away quietly to rejoin our convoy assembling in Table Bay. Morning found us steaming up the east coast of Africa towards Madagascar, where we were informed that the convoy was to split up. Until now we had all firmly believed we were still bound for Iran, but a subsequent change of orders diverted half of the ships to Bombay in India, and the remainder, including the *Warwick Castle*, headed across the Indian Ocean for an unknown destination. We had followed the course of the Japanese advance in Malaya on the radio but the guarded nature of the broadcast reports gave us no clear picture of the dire emergency of the situation. The convoy called briefly at the Maldive Islands in the middle of the Indian Ocean and, now accompanied by the battleship *Resolution*, we resumed our journey.

Some days later it was announced on the ship's Tannoy that we were to be landed somewhere in the Dutch East Indies to reinforce Dutch forces against a probable Japanese attack. Finally, our reduced complement of ships moved through the Sunda Strait, between Java and Sumatra, and docked at Tandjong Priok, the port of Batavia (now Jakarta) in Java.

CHAPTER 3
Action In Java

We disembarked in the heat and humidity of Tandjong Priok harbour, close to the Equator, and got our first taste of active service in the tropics. Problems arose immediately as the full extent of the shipboard damage sustained weeks before in the North Atlantic became clear during unloading. From the *City of Pretoria*, where trucks had broken free in the hold, the crushed wreckage of dozens of motorcycles was unceremoniously hauled out, together with smashed crates of vital stores, most of them irreplaceable. The larger vehicles, too, were a sorry sight, with stove-in radiators, buckled wheels, crushed fuel tanks and splintered woodwork. As the only REME unit available, we quickly found our services in great demand for patching up all serviceable transport and other equipment before we moved inland.

The East Indies were in imminent danger of heavy air raids and probable invasion, and its anti-aircraft defences and airfields needed to be rapidly brought to readiness to counter these threats. Our main servicing base was to be in Surabaya, the naval headquarters of the Netherlands East Indies, but this was nearly a thousand miles away at the opposite end of Java. We resorted to makeshift repairs of all kinds so that as many vehicles as possible could convoy by road; even so, many essential trucks, such as mobile workshops, were too badly damaged to travel under their own power and had to be towed the whole distance. Ironically, the Suffolk Regiment had been one of the units diverted to Bombay, but their transport – several dozen Bedford trucks – was stowed on the merchant ships of our convoy. We thought we had a bonus of a few undamaged trucks, but they had to be immediately allocated to the Dutch East Indies Army, which was desperately short of troop carriers.

When our road convoy finally assembled for the journey overland, it was a miscellany of anti-aircraft guns, radar vans, mobile workshops and various commandeered civilian lorries carrying ammunition and spares. Before setting off we had hurriedly to adapt our camouflage nets to jungle conditions (the original patterns, carefully prepared before we left England, were yellow and beige for the Middle East). Where we had difficulty in obtaining sufficient material, local foliage was substituted; one vehicle even sported a large hand of bananas hanging from its bonnet! There was some consternation when we found the artic-ulated lorry commandeered for carrying high explosives was painted brilliant yellow, and we didn't have a camouflage net big enough to cover it. During the subsequent journey to Surabaya we were more than once attacked by low-flying aircraft, and the driver of this vehicle was always first out and across the paddy fields – he would certainly have qualified for the Olympic 100 metres! Miraculously, though, the truck was never hit, and he was probably in more danger squelching about in the paddy fields than if he had stayed in his cab.

Only the personnel essential to driving and maintenance accompanied the road convoy, and the rest – headquarters staff, gunners and others – went on to Surabaya by rail. I was chosen to travel with the convoy. This was to be the first of many such choices that were preordained for me that meant that I survived the war while, sadly, others did not. On the second day of the convoy we heard the sad news of our first casualties: the troop train had collided with another train a few hours after leaving Batavia – sabotage was suspected, as the responsible signalman had disappeared, and both trains had been switched onto a single track on a remote section of the railway. Some fifty officers and two hundred men were killed or seriously injured either in the accident or due to delays in mounting a rescue operation. One result of this was the immediate promotion of many officers and other ranks, as there was no question of any replacements arriving in the immediate future. So we were starting our Dutch East Indies venture at a distinct disadvantage, short of serviceable vehicles and equipment, and now with substantial casualties among essential headquarters personnel and gunnery crews.

We also had with us a large RAF contingent that had disembarked in Java, consisting of ground staff and a nucleus of pilots. None had formed part of the ill-fated rail party but they had problems of their own. Only crated aircraft had been offloaded, and the ground crews were labouring furiously to assemble them in the heat. They were also hampered by lack of facilities at the few airfields available; in the absence of proper storage, many of the crates had been dumped on the roadside, where the locals could pilfer from them.

Our road convoy experienced what was probably the most memorable journey ever for many – especially for the artillery drivers, some of whom had only six weeks training on their heavy gun-towing vehicles. They faced many hazards during the next few days, for coping with mountain and jungle conditions in tropical heat taxed even the most experienced drivers among us. Overheating (of both lorries and drivers), breakdowns, ditched vehicles, broken tow-ropes and other irritations slowed the convoy and created headaches for the REME crews, who were also having problems keeping their own transport mobile. For security reasons the convoy usually laagered for the night outside towns and villages, but, even so, we suffered problems caused by pro-Japanese natives. Under cover of darkness, and despite the presence of sentries, they would creep up and steal batteries, slash tyres or put sugar into our fuel tanks.

On the third day of our journey we reached Semarang, where the comparative comfort of a Dutch colonial barracks awaited us. Here we had the chance to service our vehicles in their work-shops and the luxury of showers and a roof to sleep under. In the evening the Dutch officers invited us to their club and plied us with Hollands gin, their staple drink. I rapidly found myself 'under the weather' and felt it prudent to return to my billet while I could still walk upright and in a straight line. The Offi-cers' Club was a large bungalow beside the main barracks playing field, and I vaguely remembered that there was a blue light over the distant gymnasium door where we were bedded down. I located this light and struck out for it in the blackout, but I was conscious of several sudden interruptions in my progress and the tendency of the dim light to disappear and return at irregular intervals. I was also aware of becoming very wet. Finally, though, I staggered into the gymnasium and fell sound asleep on the nearest palliasse. In the morning I woke to find my clothes torn and mud-stained and my body a mass of cuts and bruises. Looking across to the Officers' Club from the gymnasium doorway, I realised my nocturnal passage had taken me through a maze of barbed wire, slit trenches and other fearsome obstacles laid out as an assault course for the colonial infantry! Luckily, after a swift shower and plenty of iodine, I was able to rejoin the convoy assembling to resume our journey. (But I promised myself that in future I would avoid Hollands gin at all costs.)

Cooking on the move was nothing new; we had practised it often enough on road convoys in the UK. But it was very different in the tropics, where our unfortunate cooks had to labour over temperamental petrol cookers at the roadside in temperatures often above 100°F (38°C) in the shade, pestered by hordes of voracious flies and stinging insects ranging from the minute to the monstrous. Furthermore, all fruit and vegetables had to be immersed in a solution of potassium permanganate before cooking, to fend off an assortment of tropical diseases, while every bit of unconsumed food had to be burnt or buried, lest it sour rapidly in the humid heat and provide a breeding ground for yet more local flies. Bottled drinks frequently exploded if not kept in the shade, and the safest natural thirst-quencher was milk from fresh coconuts, a supply of which was kept in most lorry cabs. Local water was extremely suspect, even from piped supplies in towns, and it all had to be treated before consumption. We had our own 15-cwt Bedford water tanker, which supplied all our needs, its contents heavily chlorinated as a precaution against water-borne diseases. In spite of the liberal addition of de-tasting tablets, everything we drank or cooked had a disinfectant taste that only the strongest of curries seemed to suppress.

One of the major obstacles we encountered was the lack of bridges able to take the unaccustomed weight of heavy military vehicles. An advance party of Dutch Army engineers preceded us, shoring up bridges with baulks of teak and heavy bamboo. Where this was not practicable we crossed by the nearest railway bridge or viaduct. These were mainly high trestle constructions, with planks temporarily laid over the sleepers, so it was a very hairy experience crossing the deeper ravines in the mountains, particularly as the bridges had no parapets or side rails. One simply concentrated on a point on the opposite side and gingerly steered across, hoping and praying the truck wheels would stay on the planks. Those who suffered vertigo dared not look down, and by some miracle all vehicles were safely coaxed across. Guns and trailers were usually manhandled across the smaller trestle bridges which would not sustain the combined weight of the towing vehicle and its trailer.

My own vehicle, a six-wheeled Leyland workshop, grossing about twelve tons, was one of the incapacitated trucks under tow from a large Scammell recovery vehicle. It had been towed ignominiously all the way under appalling road conditions suffering six broken tow-ropes and a snapped solid tow bar. Halfway to Surabaya we went through a flooded area shortly after a torrential downpour and passed close to a riverbank. With an open cab and no windscreen, my co-driver and I could see nothing but the spray from the towing Scammell in front. Suddenly, without warning, both vehicles slid sideways and plunged into the river. A tropical river in full spate contains all manner of unmentionable pollution and is no place for the squeamish, but fortunately we could keep our heads above water by standing on the side of the semi-submerged vehicles. We were not in any immediate danger, so the main convoy did not stop, and within half an hour the 'tail-end Charlie' Scammell from our own unit which attended to convoy stragglers appeared on the scene.

Amazingly, it was only an hour before we had both vehicles winched ashore, although we had a struggle under the insalubrious water to free the towing link between them. The blistering language it provoked probably did as much to dry us out as the blazing sun which appeared after the downpour. Within an hour of retrieval from the river both lorries were dry, but we had the noisome task of clearing the interiors, which had been soaked in a mixture of river effluent, diesel oil, tinned milk and spare parts and, of course, rescuing all our personal kit. We were on our way before nightfall, though, and reached the main convoy before camping down for the night. Our comrades were pleased to see us safe and sound, but kept a respectful distance until we had had a decent bath in a nearby stream! When, after seven days, the battered convoy entered Surabaya, literally every serviceable vehicle was towing another, some having two trucks in tow. We had suffered three air attacks en route, in which one of our instrument mechanics' workshops received several tracer bullets and caught fire. There were no casualties, though, apart from one driver, who got a broken arm skidding into a tree to avoid a low-flying aircraft.

When we got to Surabaya, the artillery units took up defensive positions in and around the town and airfield, and my REME unit took over a large empty rubber factory on the outskirts to set up a major repair centre. Our immediate task was to restore all the area transport to serviceability, while our armourers, gun fitters and radar mechanics were busy maintaining the anti-aircraft artillery and setting up the highly secret radar installations we had brought with us. These were the first three field radar installations in the Far East. (The nearest similar installation was the British-made unit supplied to the US Army at Pearl Harbor. It had been the first to detect the approach of the infamous Japanese aircraft, but inexperienced operators did not interpret or believe what showed on the screen, with tragic consequences.)

By now we had learned that the Japanese advance in Malaya had ended in the surrender of Singapore, and this was corroborated by the many allied troops and refugees now passing through Java en route for Australia. It was becoming patently obvious that Java would be invaded next, and our small unit of engineers was reinforced by a detachment of Dutch Colonial mobile infantry for extra protection. We were heavily armed with rifles, sten guns, anti-tank guns and Mills bombs, but it was good to have this extra 'muscle', which relieved us from some guard duties and other defensive chores and let us concentrate on the urgent repair and maintenance needs.

The colonial troops were all Ambonese with one white Dutch officer. These troops were descended from the ancient head-hunters of the islands of Ambon and Borneo and looked a bit like Ghurkhas. After seeing their private collections of shrunken heads we were rather glad to have them on our side. They were armed with fearsome knives, called *parangs*, and sub-machine-guns and, incongruously, travelled around on Harley Davidson motorcycle combinations. After we had been in Surabaya for several days warning was given of a large Japanese convoy approaching, and preparations were made for evacuating the area.

Unfortunately, total war with all its associations came as a great shock to the residents of Java, most of whom had been used to an indolent life of tropical luxury totally unaffected by events in Europe. The coming of the Japanese had put a stop to that, but the speed of their advance had taken everyone unawares, and most Javanese were completely unprepared. To the seasoned British and Commonwealth troops, air raids and similar diversions were necessary evils to be coped with to the best of our ability. Not so for the Dutch and their colonial allies, who lapsed into chaos at the sound of an air-raid siren or a bomb dropping. On top of the general confusion there was also the fact that some residents of Dutch extraction were pro-Nazi, and the native population was influenced by Japanese propaganda.

In these confused conditions, we evacuated Surabaya late at night taking every serviceable vehicle with us. Amongst the miscellaneous transport we spirited away was a REO six-wheeled bus with only three wheels at the rear. We hadn't time to weld the damaged wheel, so the hub was lashed to the underside of the chassis with wire and the bus was driven 180 miles to our next destination.

The night journey was fraught with alarms, as the Japanese were dropping paratroops haphazardly, to coincide with invasion at three separate points in north and south Java. But our Ambonese friends soon showed their worth in rounding up one batch of Jap paratroops dropped near us. They obviously reverted to ancestral ways, for they reappeared bearing the gruesome severed heads of several Japanese. (Later on, when they too were PoWs, they showed precious little respect for their captors. The Japs confiscated their large *parang*s but stupidly did not realise that they had secreted smaller knives on their person. Many Japanese soldiers 'disappeared' into the sewers with their throats cut, and even when, as a result, patrols around the camp perimeter wire consisted of a minimum of two sentries, such was the stealth of the Ambonese that two Japanese could be talking to one another side by side one minute, and the next instant one would be dead without the other having the slightest idea who had done it. Because the Japs had no idea that there were breaches in the perimeter wire, they assumed they were under attack by local natives rather than the prisoners.)

It may seem that 180 miles is not a long way, but it took us until the following day before we finally arrived at Tilitjap on the south-west coast, after circumnavigating several roadblocks, burning villages and many abandoned vehicles. Tilitjap was a small coastal harbour full of shipping hurriedly loading personnel seeking to leave. The town was a confusion of vehicles of all types, and British, American, Australian and Dutch and refugees thronged the approach to the docks hoping to escape the impending onslaught; those among us who had experienced Dunkirk found the atmosphere in Tilitjap ominously similar. Dutch Army administration was non-existent, and the remaining Allied High command decided on a perimeter defence system to cover the maximum evacuation in the time available.

It became patently obvious that we were destined to be the rearguard, and all available anti-aircraft guns were deployed around the town, together with predictors and radar units. Altogether we mustered 16 heavy anti-aircraft guns, 50 Bofors and several hundred Bren and Vickers guns. Some three thousand Australians formed a defensive infantry perimeter outside the town, but a sizeable American field artillery regiment was hastily re-embarked within hours of landing in Java. They took all their field guns but left their motor transport in a vast park of 300 vehicles at the dockside. No attempt had been made to immobilise any of these vehicles, which still had ignition keys and full tanks of petrol, so for the short time we were in Tilitjap, transport was not a problem. In the days before Jeeps the US Army merely commandeered new cars from manufacturers' stock and stencilled a number on the bonnet, so we had the choice of Studebakers, Plymouths, Pontiacs or other popular limousines for running about the town and immediate district. When one car ran out of petrol it was simply abandoned and another collected from the docks later. Unlike their previous owners, we ensured that all abandoned transport was carefully immobilised before we left.

We did not have long to wait for the Japanese Air Force. At precisely 11 a.m. on the first morning, they came in a leisurely formation of 27 planes, the leader firing a burst of tracer as a signal to his comrades to simultaneously unload all their bombs. This was my first experience of being pattern bombed in a relatively small area. I found the sight of a shower of bombs descending at speed made one forget about the mass of hardware, take discretion for the better part of valour and make an immediate dive for cover. Unfortunately, my cover was a nearby slit trench teeming with soldier ants, which gave me a number of painful bites before it was safe to leave.

After this violent baptism, we discovered that only five vehicles remained of the 32 we had carefully parked under trees. Miraculously, apart from a few cuts and bruises, there were no human casualties, but the Japanese aircraft had suffered heavily. Most of our gunners had served in the Blitz in London and Liverpool, so found them sitting ducks and succeeded in downing 20 of the 27 that made the first raid. Two further raids that day were as predictable as the first, and the final score was 53 planes shot down. But this proved no deterrent.

Altogether, we spent a week in Tilitjap covering the daily evacuation of as many troops and civilians as the limited shipping could carry – all this in spite of daily bombing raids, some of which set fire to fuel and molasses storage depots at the docks. Now the town truly had a Dunkirk look: streets full of abandoned vehicles, burning houses and bomb craters. Large fires burned uncontrollably in the docks, and the small harbour was getting hazardous, due to sunken vessels. Japanese submarines had now circumnavigated Java and were threatening this last escape route to Australia, so finally all shipping movements from Tilitjap ceased.

In the early hours of 6 March a Japanese force was detected landing on the opposite side of the bay of Tilitjap, and preparations were immediately made for demolition and evacuation inland. Our first priority was to destroy the radar equipment – packed, complete with trailers, into the garage of a large house recently occupied by the chief of police. All the spare cathode-ray tubes and other vital parts were stacked in the rooms of the house, along with half a ton of gun-cotton and dozens of drums of diesel fuel. The resulting explosion would have done justice to any Crystal Palace firework display.

Over three hundred vehicles were immobilised or set on fire, leaving only enough lorries to evacuate the demolition teams. All the anti-aircraft guns were spiked and their tractors and ammunition limbers set on fire, full of ammunition. This was pretty risky for the demolition teams, with jagged pieces of metal, exploding shells and chunks of large lorries flying around. Later that night, as the Japanese were cautiously entering the outskirts of the town, our last troops – mostly engineers, including myself – left in three six-wheeled Austin trucks, the only remaining serviceable vehicles. Without lights, we set out for the mountains in the centre of Java, as the coastal plains were now infested with enemy troops.

That was a nightmare drive through two hundred miles of unknown territory, passing at breakneck speed through blazing villages or silent, bomb-shattered towns, being fired at by unseen groups and not knowing whether they were friend or foe, but not daring to stop to find out. We had to stop from time to time to remove hazards, including fallen trees and lethal wire ropes stretched across the road at windscreen height (this ruse and coils of Dannert wire were used by the rearguards of our own troops). In the early hours of the morning, we were halted by a road block manned by Australians, who had unfortunately destroyed a lorry load of Dutch colonial troops during the night. The Dutch wore similar uniforms and helmets to the Japanese and used similar troop-carrying trucks, so this was not surprising, and the Aussies were taking no chances. It served to underline our own good fortune in travelling so far without mishap.

After mining the road behind us the Aussies joined our small convoy with their Bedford 15-cwt truck, and we resumed our journey to the foothills. Daylight found us approaching a bridge across a ravine and we were halted by a shout from a party of Australian engineers on the opposite side bridge. They warned us not to approach as they had just activated a time charge to demolish the bridge and an explosion was imminent. Not relishing being stranded on the enemy-occupied side of the bridge, we unanimously agreed to chance a run across. All four vehicles of our convoy revved up, and we charged over the bridge at top speed, literally with fingers crossed and metaphorically with our hearts in our mouths. About thirty seconds after the last vehicle crossed, as it was furiously climbing the gradient beyond, the bridge went up with a thunderous roar, showering our trucks with far-flung debris, and its remnants fell into the valley below. Yet another close shave I had survived!

CHAPTER 4
In the Bag

The following night was uneventful, and we spent it in fitful sleep in our trucks parked under the trees of a mountain pass. Daylight saw us on the move again, and we were joined by several other service and civilian vehicles carrying a miscellaneous group of Army, RAF and Navy stragglers, mostly British and Australian, who, like us, had made for the hills to avoid the encroaching Japanese forces.

At midday this heterogeneous convoy arrived at a tea plantation in a valley about 1,500 feet above sea level. We passed through perimeter defences manned by Australian infantry and assembled near the plantation's factory buildings to take stock and have a breathing space. The location had obviously been chosen for its strategic position, as it was almost a land-locked valley approachable by only one road. We were told the Dutch East Indies government had capitulated the day before, on 8 March 1942, and that Allied officers present were deciding on a plan of action. We were disturbed by the turn of events, but most of us were unaware how critical the situation was and still thought the Allies would mount a counter-attack to retake the Indies. In fact, not only were we completely surrounded but the possibility of counter-invasion was impossible.

Escape was out of the question therefore. We comprised a mainly British and Australian combined-services force numbering well over 3,000; most, apart from the Australians, were specialist troops, many of whom had never fired a shot in anger. Knowing the reputation of the Japanese infantry, we therefore did not fancy our chances, especially as those of us who were armed were in most cases down to only five rounds per man. Typically, the Australians decided that would fight on whatever the conse-quences (most of them were hard-bitten infantry types who had recently seen service in the Middle East). Under cover of the following night, over 2,000 of these brave men disappeared into the surrounding jungle of the foothills to carry on a guerrilla war that was to last until 1945. (Alas, their ranks were decimated by disease, enemy action and treachery from native informers, and only 500 survived, having been supplied later in their campaign by secret air drops.)

Those of us who remained debated the prospects of making a break for the coast in the hope of being picked up or getting away by boat, but our future was decided for us by the approach of a Japanese staff car bearing a white flag. The Japanese realised we were in a strong defensive position, but were unaware that the bulk of the Australians had left. They knew we had a number of injured and that water and food were in short supply, and as an induce-ment to surrender, they announced that the war was now over for us and they were preparing internment camps for us 'based on European conditions' with access by the International Red Cross.

Not then having experienced the duplicity of the Japanese, our few officers put their heads together and, in view of our critical situation, decided to surrender, after receiving assurances from our adversaries that the wounded would have immediate hospital treatment and everyone would be accorded full prisoner-of-war status as laid down by the Geneva Conventions. The Japanese liaison officer agreed to all this, adding as a rider that if we did not surrender the Nippon Air Force would reluctantly pattern-bomb the entire valley and annihilate everyone. The following day, all arms were ordered to be stacked in a prominent pile in front of the tea plantation warehouse. (Of course, we had removed or otherwise damaged the bolts or firing mechanisms, and it is debatable whether anything left behind was useful except as scrap.) We were allowed to keep all serviceable vehicles and what little personal kit we had and ordered to proceed out of the mountains to an assembly area at Garoet, near the centre of Java, where other Allied troops who had been captured would be temporarily concentrated, before despatch to prison camps.

Garoet was also an important rail centre, and it was intended that all Allied vehicles would be parked nearby, and all prisoners would continue their journey to internment camps by rail. Such was the disruption in rail traffic, however, that we languished in a small village outside Garoet for two weeks before finally being despatched elsewhere. The village where we were interned was largely Muslim and sympathetic towards us – which was fortunate, as the Japanese had made no effort whatsoever to supply us with any food, water or medical supplies. Our hosts were brusquely ordered to shelter as many Allied PoWs as possible but such was the concentration of bodies in these small native homes that priority was given to the wounded and sick; the rest of us slept in parked trucks, outhouses or in the open. I managed to find a comfortable niche in the woodshed of a Muslim carpenter and slept soundly on a pile of fragrant sandalwood boards that he afterwards informed me were coffin panels! (I was later to come uncomfortably close to other native coffin-makers whilst in captivity, but more of that anon.)

At this time, the Japanese occupation troops were rather thin on the ground, providing only a perimeter guard around the village and leaving us very much to our own devices. Those of us in the technical services took this opportunity to surreptitiously strike back at our captors by removing various vital parts of the many vehicles parked in and around the village. Rotor-arms, coils and even batteries quietly disappeared into the muddy depths of the nearest paddy field. Some weeks after we left the village, salvage teams of PoWs returned under Japanese direction to try to mobilise these trucks, but after several days' fruitless cannibalisation it was obvious even to the dimmest Jap that none would ever be road-worthy again, and almost all were dismantled for scrap.

Garoet was our first contact, face to face, with the average Japanese soldier, and, frankly, we were not too impressed. They all appeared to be short and stocky, clad in scruffy uniforms and curious rubber-soled, canvas sided boots with separate big toes. According to their Bushido code, prisoners were despised for surrendering and considered totally expendable. Most of the troops appeared to have an aggressive manner (which we put down to a marked inferiority complex) that they advertised by furiously waving swords or rifles about. At the least provocation, they would punch, kick or rain blows on anyone unfortunate enough to be within reach, and we quickly learned to avoid them as much as possible.

When we were finally marshalled into groups for entrainment there was some distance to march to the railhead. We did our utmost to carry or otherwise assist the worst cases, but anyone who lagged behind due to incapacity was mercilessly beaten by the accompanying guards to make them keep up with the marching column. When we arrived at the station, a ramshackle train was waiting: a mix of wooden carriages and trucks pulled by two antiquated wood-burning engines. My companions and I were herded onto one of the coaches, which were fitted with wooden slatted seats running lengthways on each side. Those not lucky enough to get a seat had to sit cross legged in the central gangway. But we were better off than those in the goods trucks, which were covered and had steel sides and proved to be veritable ovens in the tropical heat.

Although it was two weeks since our capture, we had still received none of the promised food from the Japanese and had existed on native food purchased with funds shared communally by officers and men alike. Most of us still had a limited stock of British rations for an emergency, and as the rail journey was scheduled to last two days, these proved to be life-savers. For the two days I had one tin of corned beef and some Army biscuits, together with about 8oz of peanuts bought from our Muslim former hosts. As the fortunate possessor of two water bottles I had enough liquid, provided it was carefully conserved (for there was no water on the train, and no opportunity to refill en route).

The daylight hours were hot and painfully uncomfortable on the wooden slatted seats – but surely better than conditions in the steel trucks. Halfway to our destination we had to disembark where the railway ended abruptly at a blown trestle bridge and do some laborious clambering through the wreckage – down one side of the debris-littered ravine and up the precipitous other side – carrying our sick and wounded with us. Waiting for us was yet another nondescript collection of antiquated rolling stock into which we wearily collapsed before being noisily shunted away to complete our journey. Early in the evening of the second day from Garoet we clattered into Tandjong Priok, where we had first arrived in the Dutch East Indies, thus completing a full circuit of Java.

CHAPTER 5
Promises, Promises!

We formed up outside the station and marched off to what we were assured by our guards was a 'Number One Good Campo!' The exhausting two-mile trek took us through an Indonesian village where we were subjected to a barrage of abuse and missiles that only ceased when some of our escorting guards were hit and proceeded to beat off our tormentors. Our spirits fell to an all time low when we finally reached our 'Number One Good Campo'. It was reclaimed swampland with a dozen or so ramshackle shelters, each about 120 feet long by 30 feet wide, consisting of dilapidated tiled roofs supported on posts. Most of the buildings had no solid walls, and those that did needed repair. The previous occupants had left the premises in an indescribable state, with excrement, putrefying food and other unmentionable rubbish littering every square foot of floor.

We didn't look forward to our first night, but in typical British-soldier style we tried to do a bit of clearing up before bedding down as best we could. During the night we discovered that other residents of the camp included rats, bats, fleas and bugs, so the next day we launched a wholesale cleaning operation – though it was seriously hampered by shortage of water and an almost complete lack of sanitation. Conditions at this camp, the indifference of the Japs to our predicament and the unfulfilled promises of adequate food and water were typical of what we had to endure from our captors for the next three years, although we didn't know that at the time.

In the compound I was allotted to, 600 men relied on a single half-inch pipe, formerly a urinal spray, perforated with six small holes out of which dribbles of water emerged. Only by leaving half a dozen 5-gallon petrol tins under these jets day and night was it possible to collect barely enough water for all our purposes, including cooking. Drainage consisted of a single nine-inch channel running through the centre of the camp to an external storm drain, and from there to the sea. The only cleaning implements we had were some home-made straw brooms and a few spades purloined from the army vehicles left behind.

In spite of these handicaps, some semblance of order and cleanliness was eventually achieved, although we never quite succeeded in eradicating insect pests, particularly those active at night, when to the purgatory of bugs and fleas were added swarms of the malaria-carrying mosquitoes that abounded in the adjacent swampland. An improvised hospital was established in one building, and the few mosquito nets in our possession were allocated to the sick and wounded, who were still with us in spite of the Japanese promises of proper hospital treatment. By now we had begun to treat all their promises with the utmost scepticism, particularly their frequently repeated reactions that met our every request, the most common being 'Asta! Asta!' – which, like the Spanish 'manãna', meant the 'tomorrow' that never came.

Ironically, this first camp of ours was not enclosed, and one of our first tasks was erecting a barbed-wire perimeter fence to keep ourselves in! It was built under the watchful eye of a number of guards, but by taking advantage of various diversions we managed to leave certain parts of the fence unsecured, which enabled us later to make clandestine trips outside when the opportunity presented itself. Almost as soon as the perimeter fence was complete and a guardroom had been built, our captors began to draft parties of prisoners onto daily work details outside the camp. As their daily demands for fit men became more insistent, only the sick or disabled were left to look after the camp.

Despite obstacles the buildings were finally made more habitable, and drawing on my pre-war occupation as a plumber, we built latrines and improved the water supply, but the ubiquitous mosquito still returned to plague us at night. Grudgingly, the Japanese augmented our dwindling food reserves with some rice and soup. The rice was usually the residue from bombed warehouses at the docks, swept up from the floor or retrieved from damaged sacks by PoW parties loading ships, so we often found broken glass, nails, maggots and other debris in it when it reached our cookhouse. After diligent straining had removed the worst of the rubbish the resulting gooey mess provided two meals, approximating to one army mess tin in total. We did not particularly care if the straining did not remove all the debris – when you are hungry, you put up with practically anything that is set in front of you, even if the consequences, like the food, might not be altogether palatable. That a smell of oil pervaded our food did not matter in the least; we needed to eat what was provided or starve – beggars can't be choosers.

Our captors provided no cooking facilities whatsoever, so we made improvised stoves of bricks and iron bars, and driftwood and salvaged timber for fuel were acquired by working parties from derelict buildings outside the camp and from the adjoining sea shore. Forty-gallon steel oil drums were laboriously cleaned out and used to cook both the rice and the inevitable soup. The latter was based on sea water collected by daily ration parties. The salt content was an essential part of our meagre diet, as were the sundry shellfish and strips of seaweed that appeared now and again, although the soup was usually a lukewarm watery mixture derived from Chinese cabbage or other insipid oriental vegetables 'flavoured' with a microscopic portion of pork. The daily ration for the whole camp (at that time numbering 3,500 inmates) was one wild pig, which for obvious reasons was used in its entirety, down to the twirl in its tail! Working parties gave us the opportunity to 'acquire' and smuggle into camp various additions to our diet, but it was a chancy business, involving a beating-up by the guards and confiscation of the hard-won spoils if discovered. Later, gardens were started within the camp, where the prolific soil and warm climate produced a variety of vegetables – but finding the seeds to grow them from in the first place was a constant problem.

The early months of captivity were undoubtedly the worst, particularly for the many not acclimatised to the tropics (including all us Brits), and we inevitably suffered from shortages of vitamins and protein. On top of this, we had long hours of back-breaking work in temperatures that often reached 120°F (49°C) in the shade. Inevitably this took its toll, and in a camp population with no medical supplies and insufficient food, malnutrition and tropical diseases appeared. Over two hundred men died from malaria, dengue fever, dysentery or beriberi in the first six months.

———✦———

Malaria is still a killer in third-world countries today. Wherever there is water and warm humid conditions, there is the ever-present high-pitched whine of the female *Anopheles* mosquito, whose bite injects parasites into the blood stream. These penetrate the red blood cells, grow and then burst out to attack other healthy cells. There are three stages to a malarial attack – the cold stage, the hot stage and the sweating stage. The first lasts only about an hour; the second, when the body temperature might rise to 106° F (41° C) with accompanying headaches and delirium can last several hours; the final stage of sweating is accompanied, eventually, by the headaches becoming less marked and the patient feeling decidedly better – until the next attack that is. The frequency of the attacks depended upon the type of fever – for some it could be every third day, for others every second day; the most severe attacks could occur within hours of the last. It really was a matter of luck, in the end, whether you rode the attacks or they killed you. Even today it takes me far longer to get rid of a cold because of residual malaria that, once contracted, is never fully eradicated from the body.

Dengue fever, also known as breakbone fever, is also transmitted by mosquitoes. It is a sudden and short infectious fever characterised by swelling and pains in the joints. The unfortunate victim would be covered in a rash, which would be followed by stiffening of the joints. After about three days the symptoms would pass off, only to recur two or three days later. A third, or even fourth, relapse might follow, and it could be months before the pain in the joints subsided. Dengue fever might not be a killer in itself, but it left men in a weak condition, and if they were then were forced onto work parties rather than recuperating, then that usually did for them.

Dysentery was also ever-present. Once one person caught it, it could spread like wildfire because of the insanitary conditions we were forced to endure. It had an incubation period of one to seven days, so you would never know whether you had been in contact with someone infectious. No matter how hard we all tried to keep clean, the shortages of water made it inevitable that dysentery would take hold almost anywhere we went. The symptoms varied from mild diarrhoea to acute nausea with perforation of the intestine and haemorrhage of the gut. The mortality rate could be frightening, especially when the Japs would not provide adequate medicines to ensure a person's survival

If all this was not enough, the so called 'fit' survivors did not escape unscathed. Practically everyone suffered from tropical ulcers or similar skin complaints, with prickly heat and heat stroke daily occurrences on working parties. Tropical ulcers were an almost inevitable result of any cut, open sore or wound. Bacteria, mostly in the soil, would attack any break in the skin, literally eating away the flesh down to the bone in the most severe cases. In the absence of essential drugs such as sulphadiazine, our doctors could only attempt to keep the infection at bay with drastic treatment such as Epsom salt poultices. In spite of this, many PoWs suffered permanent disfigurement and often amputation, and the situation did not improve much until the Japanese released pitifully small quantities of Red Cross medical supplies during the later years of our captivity.

When the war ended, a vast store of Red Cross food parcels, medical supplies, clothing and mail dating back to 1943 was discovered at Yokohama. There was no reason why these life-saving supplies should not have been distributed, and one can only conclude that withholding them was deliberate policy on the part of our captors, who regarded us as expendable anyway. A tragic aftermath of this discovery was that much of the dormant mail from PoWs to their loved ones was forwarded by the US postal authorities, who could not have known that the mail was not current, and much of it had been deliberately with-held by the Japs for over two years. As a result, after Japan's surrender some dependants received back-dated mail from PoW sons who had long since gone to their graves and were never to return to England.

—*—*—

Plagues of flies were our biggest disease-spreading menace, and the Japanese would instigate 'fly-catching' sessions in an attempt to lessen their loathsome numbers. Five cigarettes were offered as an inducement for every fifty flies killed, and as a result a 'racket' arose. Cigarettes were part of the camp currency, as at that time we received no payment whatever for our press-ganged services. It was the practice for prisoners to report to the guard-room with a quota of dead flies, which, once counted, was consigned to the rear of the guardroom where a prisoner-of-war orderly was supposed to burn the remains. He would smuggle back a substantial number of them to us, and the following day they would be produced again to the unsuspecting Jap quartermaster. When their quota of cigarettes ran out and the fly population seemed as prolific as ever, an abrupt halt was called to the scheme!

———

Demands for daily working parties became more and more insistent, particularly when they were affected by illness, which the Japanese did not consider a sufficient excuse to avoid working. Initially they decided to halve the rations of the sick, and then, when this did not have the desired effect, they cut them altogether. The remaining 'fit' men still working therefore had to share their rations with those left in camp, resulting in less food for themselves. This, of course, produced a vicious circle, resulting in yet more sick, many of whom were forced to keep working in order to receive sufficient food. The situation, though grim, made everyone even more determined to survive and outwit our captors, and efforts were redoubled to smuggle both food and medical supplies into the camp. In this way, we were able to keep going until a change in the camp's Japanese administration brought some improvements, though nothing of real significance.

Daily working parties usually began early, as the sun rose, and most lasted ten hours. Tasks varied from bomb-damage clearance, road repairs and loading ships to salvage parties recovering vehicles and armaments which had been scattered over a wide area after the surrender. Arduous though these activities were, they provided a welcome break from the monotony of camp life and gave us the opportunity to scrounge – something we became very good at. In spite of the heat and flies and the ever-present harassment from guards, we were nevertheless able to see the funny side of some of the situations we found ourselves in. A sense of humour was a decided asset and helped to keep one sane, and indeed alive, under extremely trying circumstances.

The inescapable fact was that we were all prisoners of a very cruel and unpredictable enemy, living in conditions no self-respecting person would expect an animal to have to endure. We were almost twelve thousand miles from home and completely out of touch with friends or families for at least the first eighteen months of captivity. No Red Cross supplies reached us until early 1944, after we had been prisoners for two years, even though we learned later that they had been sent almost as soon as the news of our capture had been received. Immediately they arrived such supplies were purloined by the Japs for their own use. Had we had some of these rations, then we would have been fitter and more able to carry out the tasks our captors required, and they would have had fewer sick people on their hands. They did not seem to appreciate the logic of this and were totally unconcerned that their actions were causing deaths every day. We subsequently discovered that at home we had been posted as 'missing believed killed' and, worse, our indifferent captors did not issue any details of the number of Allied prisoners to the International Red Cross until mid-1943. By this time many more had died in captivity than had been killed in action.

One of our early tasks was to salvage as many vehicles as possible, both military and civilian, and assemble them on a nearby airfield for cannibalisation and repair. Japanese communications all over the south-west Pacific were so stretched that every available serviceable car or truck was hurriedly patched up and shipped away to the many combat areas. It was strictly against the Geneva Conventions for prisoners to be employed on any task directly associated with the enemy war effort, but this did not seem to worry our captors. Our way of getting some of our own back for this inhuman treatment was to take every possible opportunity we could for some quiet sabotage.

We took full advantage of any lapse in supervision by our guards when we were cannibalising the miscellaneous vehicles. The percentage of roadworthy vehicles resulting from our efforts was very low, and those that were finally driven to the docks usually had some inherent fault carefully fixed so that any subsequent damage would occur far from our assembly area, and preferably on the field of battle, to the discomfiture of the drivers. We took some comfort from the fact that no vehicle that we were able to 'deal with' would last very long.

To say that any sabotage or subversive activity was severely discouraged was an understatement; the Japanese Command had drawn up a set of rules designed to deter us, ranging from long terms of solitary confinement to death by beheading or shooting. As these punishments were inevitably also preceded by a severe beating and torture, one was careful to cover one's tracks to avoid any direct involvement. Inevitably, though, when PoWs were suspected of instigating damage our captors would resort to collective punishment, and this proved very unpopular amongst fellow sufferers, who often had no idea that the sabotage was being perpetrated. Needless to say, British and Australian prisoners could be relied upon to keep mum and suffer in silence but this attitude was not always apparent in some of our allies, notably the Indonesian prisoners and some pro-Nazi Dutch – whom we swiftly learned not to trust, and who would try to shift the blame onto us to avoid being punished. Despite the hazards, though, every possible subterfuge and clandestine activity was pursued under the very noses of our captors; this served to relieve our frustration and enabled us, indirectly, to contribute to the Allied War effort within the limits of our prisoner of war existence. I certainly did my bit whenever possible right up to the end of the war, and I know that what I did certainly would have saved lives, even if my own was put under threat by doing it.

<hr />

Among many other impositions, we were forced to sign an under-taking not to escape – again contrary to international agreement. Escape, however, was probably the last of our options, as the odds were so heavily stacked against us. Even if we could have secured a boat and the necessary provisions, the daunting prospect of crossing hundreds of miles of shark-infested ocean regularly patrolled by enemy aircraft and submarines was enough to deter the bravest. Several ill-fated attempts were made, but in almost every case the disparity in height and looks between Europeans and Asiatic people made daytime movement impossible, and the native population of Java and the surrounding islands would soon betray such escapees, either for a reward or to avoid Japanese retribution for assisting PoWs. All known cases of recapture ended in summary execution by shooting or decapitation.

In spite of long hours of backbreaking toil and limited rest, time could drag interminably, with little reliable news from the outside world and no visible end to our captivity. The bane of our existence was the inevitable rumour-monger, who would recount the most varied and improbable tales of Allied successes elsewhere, often followed by an suggested impending invasion of our area and the probability of release. Starved as we were of the truth, we tended to grasp at any snippet of hopeful information, and it took a strong mind to discount these wild stories – which often had a depressing effect on the sick and dying among us when eventually proved utterly groundless.

Apart from the overriding preoccupation of getting enough food and trying to keep fit and disease-free in the adverse conditions, we explored other means to try and take our minds off the current situation. One day in ten was usually declared a *yasume*, or day of rest, when, apart from carrying out essential chores, we could indulge in recreational activities. We made improvised games, laboriously hand-painting scrap cardboard to provide decks of cards, and some very professional chess and draughts sets were carved out of local hardwood using army pocket knives, razor blades and broken glass. Chess tournaments, whist drives and rubbers of bridge were very popular, and, after a pitch was roughly levelled, our fitter members even played football. The Japanese themselves took an interest in the inter-compound matches, and once asked us to play a team made up of the prison guards. This 'friendly' match soon deteriorated into a rugby scrum during which the 'visitors' came in for some extremely rough treatment. In spite of our assurances that it was all part of the game, our captors did not bother to ask for a return match!

Other than the infrequent football matches, most other gatherings of more than five were frowned upon except for the 'Tenko' (Japanese for 'roll call') parades and inevitable food queues at meal times. In spite of these restrictions, activities in the huts could exceed the permitted number if one had enough look-outs. As a result, lectures, quiz programmes and even some music was possible to while away long evenings. Several interesting talks, in which the speakers described their civilian occupations, resulted in some fascinating insights into how the other half lived – including one of our pack who was a professional burglar, and whose nefarious background actually helped us in wartime, with lock-picking and other such activities.

One memorable occasion on which all his skills were put to the test occurred after one of our frequent visits to Tandjong Priok docks to clear out bomb-damaged warehouses. Whilst engaged in this task we came across a cardboard carton containing 10 large tins of Carnation condensed milk. This we knew would be manna to the medical orderlies looking after our chaps, especially for the dysentery sufferers. We hid the carton, we thought, from prying eyes. Having got it past the gate guard we were progressing towards the medical area when we were stopped in our tracks by the Guard Commander.

His more thorough search of what we had retrieved that day soon resulted in the discovery of our precious cargo. He promptly confiscated it, whilst also severely berating the gate guard who had allowed it through. Although the Guard Commander indicated to us that the hoard would be shared with his men, we knew him to be such a selfish individual, with little respect for either us or his men, that he would not allow that to happen. No, the only throat down which that precious nectar was likely to go was that of the Commander. We went back to our huts feeling dejected.

However, soon the news of this 'theft' of our milk reached the ears of one in our midst who was a 'self-confessed' burglar in peacetime but who was always prepared to use his skills for the benefit of his fellow PoWs in wartime. The forces call up made no distinction between people or their peacetime professions at the lower levels of society and the odd rogue who lived on his wits could be found in most parts of the army, navy or air force.

The PoW who that day had been detailed as 'general dogs-body' at the guardroom later reported that the carton was now under lock and key in the food store which was an extension to the guards' sleeping quarters in a separate timber building at the rear of the guardroom. The sleeping quarters were accessed by an external door, leading to two rows of tatami straw beds. Between these was the padlocked access door to the food store. All these details were gleaned from our 'insider' by our 'ex burglar' who, after just a few moments consideration, volun-teered to retrieve the contents of the carton from its resting place that very same night.

With an assistant to cover his access and return through the perimeter wire and carrying a straw sack (as any self respecting burglar does of course!) he first watched carefully for the passing of the two sentries and then quietly and successfully entered the side door of the guards' sleeping quarters – this was thankfully always kept open so that any of the guards caught short during the night could access the outside latrine. Crawling silently between the sleeping forms of the eight guards that were normally in the room, he proceeded to pick the padlock of the food store, closed it behind him and as silently as possible transferred all 10 milk tins into his sack, leaving behind the empty carton.

Carefully opening and then closing the door and padlocking it, he once again crawled between the tatami bunk beds. This time that journey was fraught with more danger as he had to go as slowly as possible to ensure that none of the tins hit one another and give his presence away to the snoring throng. Once again checking that the two sentries had exchanged waves and passed on, he regained the inside of the camp and immediately reported to the camp hospital. Here he recommended that the tins were individually buried until after the expected reprisals concerning their theft were over.

On the following morning all hell was let loose as the guard commandant went to avail himself of the first of his Carnation treats and found only the cardboard shell. Not unnaturally, he would never have suspected that we had in our midst one so expert in theft literally under the noses of the guards and they were all roused from their beds and immediately accused of this heinous theft! His reaction was both brutal and predictable. Thus the few early risers in the camp were treated to the spectacle of every one of the bleary eyed guards beaten with the judicious use of a baseball bat to extract a confession from one or more of them as to who had stolen his stolen goods!

Later we heard that their tatami beds had all been completely ripped apart and that these luckless and by now severely bruised guards had also been ordered to dig out the contents of their latrine in an endeavour to trace the missing tins. Bemused prisoners could only look on with incredulity at that morning's events, not knowing what all the fuss was about. Whilst secretly warmed inside at the beating their captors were suffering, they were all the while concerned at the natural reaction of the guards to take out their anger on any PoW. Indeed for some weeks after this incident, life proved to be somewhat unpleasant for both the guards — who had been accused of the theft and continued to be under suspicion — and the PoWs, as the guard commander continued to search high and low and administer the occasional beating to get rid of his obvious anger.

What was particularly pleasing was the later effect of adding the milk to the diet of the dysentery patients. Our man's prompt action was certainly much appreciated by the camp medical staff, who would often see a visible difference in their patients after its use. The subsequent addition to our dock visit 'maintenance staff' of our ex-burglar friend resulted in a number of other clandestine operations over time and his skills at cat burglary never ceased to amaze us.

The details of his particularly audacious exploit with the milk were kept secret for many weeks, even from other PoWs, who by that time included a number of Indian, Eurasian and other non-British prisoners. These particular individuals could not always be trusted to keep a secret, especially if there was a reward offered for any information. A number of them would have no compunction in snitching on a British PoW if they felt that might give them a trusted status with our guard commander. He never once suspected any of us and we left the camp secure in the knowledge that the treatment meted out to some of our boys over the time we were in Tandjong Priok was in part compensated by the beatings he gave his own men. It didn't matter to us one iota that every one of them was innocent and would never have had a clue as to what had happened. They were almost certainly unaware of the existence of the milk in the first place.

What happened subsequently to our ex-burglar colleague I cannot tell you. After all this time I don't even recall his name and I have no idea if he survived the brutalities of being a PoW or, if he did, whether on his return he went back to his old ways or turned over a new leaf. If the former then I do pity those who lived close by to him – if he could do what he did in such extreme circumstances, tackling a suburban British house would have been an absolute doddle!

I'd like to think and hope that he did survive and got a proper job for there is no doubt that this particular action was one of great bravery as well as bravado on his part. For there is little doubt that, had he been discovered at any stage of his journey, but more especially with his bag of swag, the wrath of the guard commander would have known no bounds. I have no doubt that we fellow prisoners would have been forced onto the parade ground not to see him receive a beating with a baseball bat but to witness him being beheaded.

———✦———

Whilst this man was something of a hero, that could certainly not be said about one in our midst. Again I don't recall his name but I do remember him being from the London area. This individual would have sold your soul to the devil if he had half the chance and keep the proceeds. He volunteered, with no previous experience, to be one of our hospital orderlies but we later found that helping his fellow prisoners was not the underlying motive. He would steal some of the medicines and pills that were in his charge and then sell when they were most needed by those in the hospital. There is little doubt that, had some of our men had half a chance they would have bumped him off within the camp, so hated an individual did he become. Bbefore that could happen he went on one of the drafts but rather than sticking with us he latched onto a number of Americans. When sent up to the infamous railway, he once again offered to be a hospital orderly and carried on the same business as before, in conditions where the needs in the hospitals were even more pressing.

However, his nefarious activities did not go unnoticed by those he had been drafted with. After the war we heard that he was on the train taking those who survived the railway to liberation, and was seen sitting at ease on the rear balcony, with legs dangling over the side (no doubt with his pockets full of the money he had 'earned' during his time in the various camps). Some time later, after the train had gone over a deep ravine, he was no longer sitting on the balcony but had disappeared. Readers can form their own opinions as to who carried out this deed and it certainly would not have been the Japanese – whether he survived or not I have no idea but I very much doubt it. The extended suffering he had caused to fellow prisoners by stealing vital medicines had clearly not gone down well with others in the camp and his comeuppance was both swift and, sadly, fully deserved.

CHAPTER 6
Bogor 'Hospital'

Many and varied were the tasks we were expected to perform both inside and outside the camp – which, even the Japanese began to realise, needed better facilities if it was to sustain sufficient working parties. With every project our captors impressed us into, we came to appreciate how the Pyramids were built: with slave labour – for that was what we really were! The Japanese seemed to believe that superhuman effort alone would achieve miracles, even when assisted by only the minimum of food and materials and the most primitive tools.

I became involved in providing adequate drains and latrine buildings, and several weeks of laborious work saw a marked improvement, with some control over the fly population as a result. However, the working conditions of the drainage team were, deplorable to say the least, especially since we had no soap or disinfectants. So, paradoxically, one after another we all succumbed to the very diseases we were trying to eradicate. Both inside and outside working parties became so depleted by sickness, that even our guards became alarmed at the thought of contagion and instituted a series of mass inoculations. A team of Japanese medics descended and proceeded to treat everyone in camp, starting with the returning work details. The vaccination was painful and primitive: one was scored on the upper arm with the prongs of a broken pen nib, and then some dubious-looking vaccine was squeezed into the cuts and rubbed in with a communal piece of no-longer-white cotton wool. This agonising performance was repeated until the pen nib became too blunt and was changed for another. Remarkably, no one contracted blood poisoning – probably all our antibodies were themselves so highly charged with tropical bugs that any further poison introduced was doomed to extinction!

I had been inoculated and, later in the day, began to feel extremely woozy. I was now collared by a patrolling guard, who assumed I was one of the incoming work party – no amount of protestation would convince him that I was working inside the camp – and in my bemused state, I was forced to join the queue for another dose of vaccine. Within minutes I had collapsed; friends whisked me away to our billet and. not until two days later did I return to some semblance of normality. Apparently, though, without ever being conscious of doing so, I had attended every roll call (covered by friends answering on my behalf) and eaten any food put before me, all the while staring blankly into space!

Shortly after this, a severe bout of malaria finally caught up with me, brought on by constant exposure to the hordes of mosquitoes that abounded around the drains we were digging through the swampy soil. Our taskmasters did not consider malaria on its own a sufficient excuse to stop work, but I had acquired several other equally debilitating complaints; dengue fever was causing severe headaches and affecting my sight; I also had a tropical ulcer on one ankle which refused to heal and a microbial skin complaint under the arms and legs, which made mobility extremely painful. Finally, I succumbed to a bout of dysentery, which entailed an average of twelve visits to the nearest latrine every twenty-four hours. The small team of dedicated doctors and orderlies in our makeshift hospital were hopelessly overworked, but still managed to perform miracles of healing and surgery with severely limited drug supplies and improvised surgical equipment. My treatment consisted of one quinine tablet a day (smuggled into camp by some brave soul) and a diet of watery rice mixed with powdered charcoal. No other medication was available, but my condition was steadily worsening, so it became apparent that there was little more the camp doctors could do for me.

It was the practice to send all critical cases to the nearby town of Bogor, where there was said to be a Japanese military hospital that was prepared to accept a limited number of prisoner patients. We had sent some fifty serious cases to this 'hospital', but after a few weeks only ominous bundles of personal effects had returned to our camp to indicate their fate. Fortunately, I didn't know this – and wasn't in a fit state to understand it if I had been, for my waking hours were interspersed with bouts of delirium and high fever that left me soaked in perspiration and utterly exhausted. From my lucid moments, I remember being laid on the flatbed of a three-ton truck and watching the road rush past the rear axle through a broken floorboard as it bumped its way to Bogor some fourteen miles away. When we reached a building surrounded by a high stone wall I was placed on the grass verge, and the lorry sped off, leaving me unattended in the blazing sun. I have no idea how long it was before someone emerged from a small door in the wall to carry me in, but I vaguely made out the figures of two Dutch orderlies, who finally deposited me in a tiled room occupied by several other inert forms.

This so called 'military hospital' turned out to be a botanical school/gardens commandeered by the Japanese as a satellite hospital for prisoners of war. (A couple of the Japanese in charge of these gardens were botanically minded, and they did at least attempt to keep their fellow troops from cutting down the many trees and plants for fuel: it is thanks to them that the gardens exist to this day.) The resident doctor, Dr Hekking, was not a medical man at all, but a qualified botanist who had been retained by the Japanese merely because he was a 'doctor' of botany. Fortunately for most of the PoWs in his charge, he practised a homeopathic treatment based on herbs and plants which was instrumental in saving many lives, mine included, and for those whom he was unable to cure he made the remainder of their lives more bearable.

The room I found myself in was about twenty feet square and contained twelve other patients beside myself. With one exception, we slept on flat boards or doors laid on the tiled floor (and the only bedding or blankets were those we brought with us). The exception was an iron bed in the corner, which (it was soon obvious) was reserved for the most serious case in the ward. Those room mates who were in a fit state to talk told me that everyone present was suffering from one terminal complaint or another. Next to me was a young officer with tuberculosis and diphtheria, who was soon to occupy the iron bed. Each night an unfortunate occupant died, and a rough coffin was made in the adjoining room by two native carpenters, usually at night to avoid disturbing patients elsewhere in the hospital.

Across the passage from this room was a security ward where violent patients were confined. At the time of my admission it contained a sergeant in the last stages of dengue fever. Without proper treatment he was now blind and had become deranged, recounting all his past life in a loud voice during the small hours of the night.

Coupled with the nocturnal manufacture of coffins and the nightly demise of another room occupant, these ravings did little to improve one's outlook on life, and those of my waking hours not marred by delirious fantasies were unashamedly spent in fervent prayer. On the twelfth day after entering hospital I found myself the sole occupant of the room, all the others having succumbed and been whisked away at nightfall. At midnight I awoke to hear the usual hammering in the next room and realised another coffin was being made in anticipation of my demise – they had not missed a night without a customer for the past two weeks. However, my prayers must have been answered, as around 3 a.m. I heard the creak of a bamboo stretcher, and the two Dutch orderlies passed the doorway with an inert body between them.

A few moments later one of the orderlies put his head round the door and asked how I was feeling. I told him my feelings would improve considerably if my accommodation was changed, and the sooner the better. He confided that there had been a sudden death elsewhere in the hospital and suggested that I fill the vacant place. This was done, and when the Japanese held the morning roll call it was assumed that it was the occupant of the end room who had died, as the count tallied correctly elsewhere. (Fortunately for me, most Europeans looked the same to a Jap, just as most of them looked alike to us, and the changeover was not noticed. At that time only the Allied administration bothered to keep records of prisoners – all the Japanese were interested in were numbers.) The place I had been moved to was one the Jap guards tried hard to avoid, as it was the ward with those who had venereal disease; the Japs were frightened to death of catching VD. This all helped to make my progress back to reality a bit less of a problem, as they rarely bothered us in that room.

The accommodation elsewhere in the Botanical-School-cum-hospital was cleaner, and some improvement on Tandjong Priok camp. With the addition of several nutritious herbs to augment the rice diet, and freedom from hard work, my condition began very slowly to improve. Proximity to the city of Batavia meant that a small supply of drugs was regularly smuggled into the hospital – never enough, but a godsend nevertheless. We discovered that a Eurasian chemist was responsible for arranging these clandestine deliveries, to both the botanical school and the distant camp. The Japanese never discovered him providing this life-saving help, and he operated strictly on an IOU basis with the British and Dutch governments, for which he was amply reimbursed at the end of hostilities.

Although we were not greatly troubled by guards, there was the daily ordeal of the visiting Japanese medical officer's inspection. All patients capable of standing, however uncertainly, were expected to parade each morning, when he would pass from one to another prodding with the billiard cue he invariably carried. Anyone who failed to bow in his presence promptly got a crack on the head with the heavy end of it, with many unfortunates suffering thus because they were just too ill to realise what was going on. The Japanese medical officer knew this full well and took a perverse delight in administering this brutal and unnecessary punishment. Eventually those he considered fit to leave were consigned back to their camps, as the commandants expected him to provide replacements for the depleted working parties.

Although far from fit and a shadow of my former self, I returned to Tandjong Priok camp to discover that, in my nine-week absence a large draft of PoWs had left for Borneo, amongst them the majority of my own unit. For them, it was 'out of the frying pan, into the fire'; I learned later that most had perished in the terrible conditions in Kuching Camp, which culminated in a forced march that has been written about elsewhere. The remnants of my unit left in camp – thirteen, including me – were too sick to accompany the draft, which saved our lives. Together with the sick and disabled prisoners, we formed a maintenance depot and central cookhouse, as the camp was destined to become one of the main transit camps in Java.

During the next year, the inmates of most of the smaller camps passed through Tandjong Priok en route for a variety of destinations, most of them with conditions infinitely worse than those in the Dutch East Indies. These drafts consisted of all types of Allied servicemen: American, Australian, Indian, Dutch and Indonesian, together with several merchant seamen who had been offloaded by German raider ships operating in the South

Atlantic and Indian Ocean. Most of the merchant seamen had been well treated by their German captors, and under their new oriental taskmasters it came as a great shock to be forced to endure the primitive conditions that had become a way of life, and death, for us. One unfortunate RAF gunner had been rescued from a shot-down Catalina aircraft, operating out of Gibraltar, by a German raider ship en route to the South Atlantic. From the relative luxury of an RAF base, whence he could fly home to Britain on 48-hour leave, he was transported thousands of miles to the other side of the world and ended up a prisoner of the Japanese.

While I was in hospital, the Commandant of the camp had been replaced by another, who was slightly less harsh in his outlook. The guards, too, had changed and were provided by units recently in action – prison-guard duties being regarded as something of a rest for them. The guards (and their Commandant) rarely stayed for more than three months before being posted away, usually accompanying drafts of PoWs. As a result, the camp administration was largely left to the British, who preserved a wary rapport with each succeeding influx of Japanese. By this time most of us had become acclimatised to a tropical existence the hard way and were starting to understand what made our captors tick. Everyone was becoming expert at scrounging and improvisation, and it was harder for any Japanese to outsmart us.

Curiously, our captors regarded us as the most honest and fair-dealing of their polyglot range of prisoners and would accept our word against any Dutch or Indonesian. This could obviously be useful in extricating ourselves from potentially difficult situations and did not always endear us to the former, amongst whom we discovered a number of informers. (What these despicable people hoped to gain from spying and reporting on fellow prisoners is debatable – they still suffered the same conditions as we all did, and were openly despised by the Japanese anyway.)

Our food, though never very plentiful, was now augmented by several prolific gardens within the camp. We were not allowed livestock, although one of the Commandants did start an experimental (and short-lived) poultry farm. It was run by six 'qualified poultry farmers' from among the PoWs. (The nearest relevant skill any of them had was boiling, poaching or scrambling an egg, but that did not stop them tackling their new task with gusto!) Although accompanied by a guard on their daily rounds, they regularly smuggled out all the eggs that were laid and gave our hospitalised patients a much needed treat. After several weeks with no eggs forthcoming for the Japanese, the ringleader of the 'poultry' prisoners managed to convince the Commandant that the birds were suffering from lack of protein, and subsequently secured a daily sack of rice polishings, chillies and other 'essential' vitamins – which, like the eggs, were quickly diverted into our camp hospital.

All good things come to an end, though, and having of all those juicy fowl strutting about was too tempting for some hungry prisoners. The chicken farm was outside the main prison compound, but several forays were made under cover of darkness via the concealed 'weak points' in the wire fence, and roast chicken featured on the menu. When it became obvious even to the Japanese that their flock was diminishing, they checked throughout the camp, but not so much as a feather remained as evidence; instead ample clues were left around the poultry house to indicate that local natives had broken in during the night. Finally the Japs gave up the poultry farm as a bad job.

———

Until the time of the first drafts we still had a number of padres among us, who, under very difficult circumstances, endeavoured to fulfil our spiritual needs. Apart from the ridicule that they were subjected to by their captors, assemblies of more than five men were forbidden at any time, except for the occasional concert party or the ubiquitous working parades. Nevertheless, one of the more lenient Commandants finally granted permission to hold church services, and even to build a replica church. The finished chapel was a labour of love by a small band of dedicated Christians who produced marvels of carved woodwork. One of our number, Lieutenant Commander Upton RNVR (who in peacetime worked for Cable and Wireless on ships laying communication cables between the islands) even produced two beautiful stained-glass windows for it.

Considering that all the materials had to be either prised out of the reluctant Japs or literally stolen from buildings outside the camp, it was a minor miracle that our little church was finished. Like many other projects during our prisoner-of-war existence, we were not able to enjoy its benefits for long. Late in 1943 all padres were deported to Formosa (now Taiwan) to work in the copper mines, and we were left without any religious influence except for one or two dedicated lay preachers who remained.

In spite of all the improvements made during our stay in Tandjong Priok, it still remained a very unhealthy place, as the adjoining military cemetery testified. In the latter stages of 1943 the camp was finally closed, and those of us left were transported to a camp in the foothills of Java where the climate was a little more amenable. Tandjong Priok Camp was subsequently bull-dozed and redeveloped after World War II, and no trace remains of the original buildings. The stained-glass windows of the original camp church were salvaged, though, and are now in All Saints Anglican Church in Jakarta.

———

There was a postscript to this episode on 15 August 2005, during the celebrations of the 60th anniversary of VJ day. At the age of 86, as the last surviving person to have helped build the church at Tandjong Priok, I was privileged to take part in a ceremony to dedicate replicas of Lieutenant Commander Upton's stained-glass windows – they are now on display at the National Memorial Arboretum at Alrewas in Staffordshire in the beautiful Far East Prisoners of War Building that commemorates all my PoW colleagues who lost their lives during or after the war. The windows honour the four nations incarcerated in the camp – British, Dutch, Australian and American – and while the replicas were being made the artist noticed something about the features of the lion rampant in the British section of the window. Closer inspection revealed that Lieutenant Commander Upton (who was involved in considerable sabotage activities in all the camps to which he was sent) had cocked a further surreptitious snook at the Japs. Unknown to them (and to many who were in the camp) the lion's face was actually that of Winston Churchill, complete with cigar!*

* The initiative for the replica window came from Meg Parkes, whose father Athol Duncan was a prisoner alongside me in the same hut in Java. When I first put pen to paper about my experiences, and met Meg, she realised that my journey paralleled that of her father, who also survived the war, and it was through this that the existence of the windows was revealed and the fund-raising needed to produce the replicas was begun. Meg has produced two books of her late father's experience from the secret diaries he kept throughout his captivity: 'Notfiy Alec Rattray... (2002) and '...A. A. Duncan is OK' (2003). She remains a great friend and is a member, like my eldest son John, of COFEPOW (Children of Far East Prisoners of War). COFEPOW's founder member, Carol Cooper, whose father never returned from the Far East, was, with her husband Ron, instrumental in fundraising for the erection and longer term maintenance of the FEPOW memorial building.

CHAPTER 7
The PoW War Effort

Many aspects of our stay in Priok camp were laced with grim humour. In the early days, the Japanese, conscious of the propaganda value of photography and anxious to create a good impression to the conquered countries in East Asia, decided to stage a banquet attended by prisoners of war and some Japanese military dignitaries in Batavia. Several fit-looking Australians were given new uniforms to wear and ushered into a large room containing a long table heaped with food and fruit and bottles of sake. A Japanese photographer set up his equipment, which included an old-fashioned magnesium flash, and prepared for the group photograph. The Aussies were warned not to touch the food, as it was to be returned after the photo session. However, the Jap photographer could not get his flash to work, and, so as not to lose face, he retired into the next room to fix it. He was gone so long that the two guards in charge of the Aussies left to see what the delay was. That was fatal; when they returned, a mere ten minutes later, with a now beaming photographer, they found their charges had cleared the board of everything edible, and then, washed it down with all the sake. Their paroxysms of rage made no impression whatever on the grinning Aussies, who shrugged off the inevitable blows with total indifference.

———⚓———

One of the few British vehicles captured intact was a Scammell recovery truck whose occupants had been overrun by invading forces before it could be immobilised. After our capture the Japanese were trying to move this prize to Tandjong Priok docks, to be shipped to their fighting forces at the front as a useful asset. No Jap driver had succeeded in mastering the vehicle's complex array of controls, so a call was put out to the PoWs assembled for salvage work. No volunteers presented themselves (although several competent diesel drivers knew perfectly well how to drive the beast), so the Japanese sergeant in charge commandeered a local Indonesian bus driver and ordered him to start the Scammell and get it moving.

The town bus service boasted a few Mercedes diesel coaches, but none so sophisticated; however, with the aid of fierce threats and prods from a rifle butt the hapless native finally managed to get the engine running. Driving the truck was quite another matter; the Indonesian was small and could hardly see through the windscreen, let alone peer over the massive counterbalance secured ahead of the Scammell's radiator. Even so, to the cheers of the Japanese guards who had clambered onto the truck, a shaky progress was made to the nearby vehicle 'park', where several roadworthy trucks awaited impending despatch to the docks.

As the Scammell entered the assembly area, it became patently obvious that the driver's vision was seriously impaired, as was his ability to steer it. After colliding heavily with several parked vehicles, the truck made a circuit of the area with the panic-stricken driver desperately attempting to brake. The clutch appeared to be stuck, and there was no way for the poor man to get the massive vehicle out of gear despite all his efforts, and those of the irate Jap sergeant. It proceeded relentlessly around the concentration of vehicles leaving mayhem in its wake and arousing panic among the guards clinging for dear life to the crane on its rear. Finally, with a resounding crash, it ran headlong into a large tree on the edge of the vehicle park, which dislodged the Jap guards on the back and dumped them in ungainly heaps on and all around. Those still on the monster tumbled off and vented their spleen on the luckless Indonesian, who ran off at the earliest opportunity. This left the furious sergeant surveying the wreckage of what was meant to have been the next shipment of serviceable transport vehicles – practically none of which was now fit to move.

Meanwhile our party of PoWs had kept a very low profile at the edge of the field, fully expecting repercussions when the fuming Jap sergeant rejoined us. Whenever the Japs suffered any loss of face (and this was a huge one), they could turn on us in an instant. There was great temptation to burst out laughing at their hilarious antics, but we all managed to keep a straight face and attempt to show concern for the men still brushing the dust out of their uniforms

'All mena!' shouted the sergeant, 'Ingrisoo truckoo, no gooda!' 'Damme! Damme! Breakoo! All finisho!'

Thank Heaven, rather than take out his ire on us, he decided the inert Scammell needed a damn good lesson, so he instructed us to smash it up – which we proceeded to do with great satisfaction. We wondered how the NCO would explain the afternoon's destruction of the rest of the transport in the 'park' to his superiors. For the remainder of the week his mood was decidedly unpleasant, and we avoided him like the plague.

———✦———

In the early days of captivity, when several parties of PoWs were engaged on vehicle salvage, life could become more than usually hazardous if we encountered booby-trapped trucks and equipment. So abandoned vehicles were approached with extreme caution: it had been common practice to conceal grenades in critical positions, or even to bury mines just in front of the road wheels, ready for unsuspecting individuals to move off. The final process of assembling all this transport and trying to make it roadworthy provided many opportunities (which we naturally took) to acquire all manner of tools, electrical equipment and other useful items to smuggle back into camp. Priority was given to any radio equipment we could find, which could be used for clandestine sets.

If vehicle bodies were burnt or damaged beyond repair, undamaged engines were removed and sent to a central motor works (formerly General Motors) in Batavia, where other teams of PoWs refurbished and overhauled them before crating them for despatch to the various combat areas as engine replacements in the field. After crating, the completed engines were carefully inspected by a civilian Jap engineer, who then gave the order to nail down the lid before passing on to the next batch of crates.

But his crucial mistake was not to stay to see the lid finally nailed down. In the few minutes before it was hammered home, untold damage could be wreaked on the engine below by cracking the china insulators on the plugs, the distributor and any other fragile parts. It took only a few seconds to remove a plug or two, put some steel filings or a few nails inside the cylinder, and then replace the plug. Nails would be driven into the windings of starter motors, electric cables severed, and sundry other tricks employed to ensure that one more engine would be useless by the time it reached Burma, or some other theatre of war.

One of the most arduous and hated chores was loading ships with fuel drums. Our enemies were short of tanker ships, and every cargo vessel that left Java was required to carry a quota of fuel for transport to the battle areas or the Japanese homeland, where supplies were severely rationed. These cargoes were potentially lethal, but it was typical of our captors that they took few precautions against the risk of fire or explosion. Hundreds of drums of every variety of oil and petrol were stacked on deck, in holds and even in companionways, making each vessel a veritable fire bomb.

The Japanese have a traditional fear of fire, and smoking was rigidly forbidden. Inexplicably, though, no other safeguards were apparent, and working parties were quick to take advantage. It was common practice when unobserved to loosen the screw caps of fifty-gallon drums (particularly those in holds) just enough to ensure that a trickle of fuel could escape. Subsequently most ships left the docks with ever-increasing quantities of highly inflammable fuel swilling around below decks awaiting the chance spark. No one will ever know how many of these floating fire hazards came to grief en route to Japan, but we did have the satisfaction of seeing one vessel erupt in flames soon after leaving harbour; probably an unsuspecting deckhand had indulged in a quiet smoke. Whatever the cause, it meant one less shipload for the enemy, and it had happened far enough away for us not to be directly implicated. We had no qualms about doing this or about the effects on the Japanese crews. It was another way we could get back at the Japs for the total disdain with which they treated us as human beings.

The curse of loading ships was that time ceased to figure in our taskmasters' calculations. Once we had started, we were often forced to finish loading a cargo so that the ship could sail the same night. This meant our already long day of ten hours' gruelling labour in the tropical heat was extended far into the night. The exhausted work parties would return to camp around midnight to collect their long-delayed evening meal of cold rice and soup and grab a few precious hours of sleep before being woken at dawn for yet another day of toil.

When I returned to camp from hospital, I was considered unfit for heavy working parties and was assigned to the camp maintenance department. (What was now one of the largest transit camps in Java required a full-time party of maintenance personnel to keep its limited facilities in some semblance of working order.) This had a reasonably well equipped workshop, with a variety of tools 'acquired' by various means outside the camp, or simply made out of available scrap. Nothing whatsoever was wasted, in case it might come in useful later (and this attitude has been part of my life ever since). Old tins, bottles and salvaged vehicle parts were recycled into every conceivable item of potential usefulness.

Under the umbrella of these activities, a great deal of clandestine work went on, including the building of several radio sets. These were ultimately concealed in a number of ingenious hiding places: one was built into the wall of a toilet block, another into the tubular frame of the Senior British Officer's bed. In addition we endeavoured to equip every outgoing draft of prisoners with a water-bottle radio.

My involvement was to adapt service water bottles by cutting them in half at the shoulder and soldering a tube under the neck. The miniaturised radio was then assembled by one of our radar mechanics, and I would then solder the bottom half of the bottle back on again. The joins were carefully filed down until almost undetectable, and the finished bottle faked with camouflage paint. An unobtrusive two-pin socket at the base of the bottle enabled a listener to plug in a single earphone (carried separately and concealed elsewhere). Because of the design of the webbing bottle carrier, any seams in the outer casing were covered, and the internally soldered tube allowed a small quantity of water to be carried, reaching to the bottle base. (This was essential, as all PoWs were expected to carry water bottles on working parties and in transit, and the guards would remove the cork and test the depth of the water with a chopstick to ensure everyone had a full bottle.) Making these radios was risky, and, had we been discovered, would have meant almost certain death.*

After careful cajoling, we persuaded the Japanese to provide us with some acid to form part of an electro-plating kit. We explained that this was for plating various hand-made surgical implements, but in reality we were making a metal rectifier installation for one of the more elaborate radio receivers. (It never occurred to our captors that the surgical instruments we had produced were of stainless steel and did not need plating. We did make a small plating apparatus, though, and 'obliged' the stream of curious guards who brought coins and lighters and other souvenirs of theirs to be 'silver plated'.)

By means of these radios – permanently tuned to Radio Delhi – we were able to discover the truth of what was happening in other theatres of war as well as in our own. But whoever listened to the radio could not tell anyone what he had heard until a week or two afterwards. If the Japs overheard us talking about anything to do with the war too soon after the event, they might realise we had clandestine radios and instigate a search, with dire consequences for anyone discovered with one of the sets. However, if they overheard us sometime afterwards, we could tell them we had heard the local natives talking in those terms. Thankfully, they were easily duped, and none of the radios I worked on in camp were ever discovered.

* A replica of the correct type of water bottle showing the part I played in its construction has been donated to the Far East Prisoners of War Building at the National Memorial Arboretum at Alrewas in Stafford-shire, and the one displayed in the Imperial War Museum in London is almost certainly one that I helped construct.

On one occasion, one of the guards appeared at our workshop in considerable distress and brandishing his rifle, which had part of the cleaning rod jammed in the barrel. Unlike a British rifle, the Japanese rifle had a long, thin steel rod complete with a bullet-shaped swivel attachment at one end for barrel cleaning. It was this bullet-shaped end that had snapped off halfway down the barrel, and the disconsolate guard was contemplating the punishment that would inevitably be meted out by his superior officer when this was discovered. We advised him that he could be in even greater trouble were he found leaving weapon in our tender care, but that, if he did indeed trust us and leave the unloaded rifle with us, it would be perfectly safe and that we would guarantee to remove the obstruction. This, we explained, would take some time, and we warned him not to be seen hanging round our workshop but to come back in about two hours.

Surprisingly, the gullible guard disappeared in the direction of the nearest native village, promising to return with a suitable reward. Once he was out of sight his rifle was subjected to some rather drastic treatment. The steel barrel was swiftly removed from the stock, heated red hot in a makeshift furnace and the stoppage violently punched out with a rusty iron rod and a large hammer. This did not improve the finely rifled bore, and the horrible score marks were erased vigorously with emery cloth wrapped around the same iron rod. Burn marks on the outside were expertly 'blued' with a mixture of charcoal and old sump oil and the barrel replaced in its stock. The woodwork was highly polished with peanut oil, and the finished article looked as if it had just been issued from the armoury. As a parting gesture, the foresight was slightly misaligned with the back sight, which rendered the weapon totally ineffective. Indeed, with the bore now considerably oversize, the rifle was likely to be much more hazardous to its user than anyone it was pointed at.

On his return, the delighted guard presented us with fifty cigarettes, a valuable form of camp currency, and promised to tell his comrades about this 'useful' service. Amazingly, during the next six months, some fifty rifles passed through our hands for this 'refurbishing', some of them from guards who really only wanted a 'new look' to their weapons. Little did they realise what was done to their prize possession, and if they subsequently killed anyone with it, that could only have been because of bad aim. Fortunately, most of them only did a three-month tour of prison-guard duty before returning to active service, so we had no repercussions.

Apart from the dodges the maintenance department got up to, most prisoners used their latent skills to the best advantage, not only in the constant battle for survival but to outwit the common enemy. Many and varied were the ruses employed, and skills from every trade and profession were put to use when the occasion demanded. Our instrument mechanics transformed cheap watches and lighters into counterfeit Rolex Oysters and Ronsons so expertly that they passed even our own critical inspection. These were bartered to souvenir-hungry Jap guards and civilian officials at exorbitant exchange rates, together with other expertly forged trade names of totally inferior quality. Cigarette lighters were of little use to us except for barter purposes, since we could not obtain petrol or lighter fuel. Nevertheless, our 'customers' regarded a spark as essential to any transaction, and our conversion 'experts' retained a few rare flints for this purpose. Replacement flints were another matter, and one ingenious PoW made several small packs of 'flints' for dispensing (at a cost) to departing guards. They were carefully prepared from the leads out of several pencil stubs by breaking them to the appropriate length. Our vendor was wily enough to ensure that only Japanese on immediate draft received these extra 'flints', as the repercussions could have been rather drastic. We would discuss all these 'dealings' in the dark of the tropical nights with considerable satisfaction and amusement while visualising the chagrin and frustration of our captors. Whether those engaged in such pursuits survived to continue them after the war, I wouldn't like to speculate!

The same PoW artists were constantly performing minor miracles in providing essential articles for camp use. These ranged from all manner of surgical instruments made from army stainless-steel cooking equipment, sterilising autoclaves from petrol cookers, right through to artificial limbs. Among the officers imprisoned was an Australian dentist who still had a pair of extraction pliers and a drill head, complete with a set of bits. We successfully built the rest of the drill using a treadle system off an old Singer sewing machine purloined from a deserted colonial home and a speedometer cable from an abandoned car. As I was involved in this, and as I needed a couple of fillings, my workmates suggested I should be the first patient. With some trepidation I offered myself to the dental officer along with the completed appliance, but, even without anaesthetics or modern cooling sprays, the experience was almost painless. In the absence of proper dental amalgam the offending teeth were expertly filled with hard dental plaster, found on one of our daily excursions. Both fillings survived until my release, when they were redrilled and properly filled by a rehabilitation dentist who commented favourably on the workmanship of the Australian PoW some three years earlier.

Also standing us in good stead were a number of formerly anti-social skills learned from those in our ranks who had been burglars, poachers and other miscreants in civilian life. Our first Christmas in camp benefited from the services of a 'moonshiner' who had produced 'poteen' in his native Ireland. We reckoned something would be needed to enliven the interminable diet of rice and overcome the absence of alcoholic drink, so the components for a still were assembled: the copper piping from an old refrigerator, a five-gallon petrol tin and a charcoal brazier. Our resident 'moonshiner' meanwhile prepared a concoction of rice, yeast, molasses, tomatoes and other dubious ingredients, which was fermented in a large carboy originally used for storing distilled water. Finally this mash was slowly distilled in the maintenance workshop and filled a collection of assorted bottles.

There were plenty of volunteers to give this 'hooch' its tasting trial, and the 'lucky' man took a sizeable swig, pronounced it 'just the job' and collapsed in a drunken stupor. Since he resisted all our attempts to revive him, we sent for one of our doctors, who diagnosed our potent brew as almost 100% pure alcohol! Our official taster did recover after some hours in the shade, albeit with a massive hangover, but, on the medical officer's advice, we diluted our 'fire water' 20 to 1 with papaya juice, and it made a welcome contribution to the Christmas Day fare. The camp cooks had also excelled themselves, producing an 'ersatz' Christmas pudding from rice, cocoa and a load of raisins smuggled in from a dockside working party. There was no turkey, of course, only the inevitable soup, which for once contained discernible shreds of meat and vegetables other than the ubiquitous Chinese cabbage. Where the extra meat came from or what its original four-footed origin was we did not bother to enquire. Some questions are better unasked.

The festive season was further enlivened by the efforts of some PoWs who made and exchanged Christmas cards and others who formed a concert party to provide an evening of entertainment. Christmas Day was the one relaxation allowed by the Japanese, several of whom occupied the front seats at the evening's variety performance. They seemed to thoroughly enjoy the antics of our performers, although fortunately the jokes were lost on them – just as well, since none of the dialogue was at all complimentary to Japan. A number of Japanese could converse in pidgin English, but even they could not follow anyone who spoke fast or in any kind of dialect. Since we also had to be on our guard against informers in our own ranks, notably Indonesian prisoners and Dutch sympathisers, we made full use of dialect, back-slang, cockney idioms or other non-standard speech when discussing anything important among ourselves. Many of the Welsh prisoners simply spoke in their native tongue and mystified everyone, including their English comrades. But we always knew their conversations in Welsh were at the expense of the Japs, whom they could abuse to their faces (while keeping a straight face themselves) without their being any the wiser!

For security reasons, the Japanese installed floodlighting on the perimeter road around the camp. Similarly, some primitive lighting was fitted in the long huts we occupied and the latrine blocks subsequently built in each compound. Lights were left on all night in latrines and the entrances to all huts to enable patrolling guards to carry out nightly checks. Lighting fires after dusk was strictly forbidden, but this did not stop PoWs from indulging in various culinary pursuits after dark. To augment the limited rations, all prisoners on working parties would seek to lay their hands on anything edible whilst outside camp. Similarly, those in camp would supplement their meals with vegetables grown in the few small patches under cultivation. To cook these items PoWs devised ingenious electrical contrivances made from discarded floodlights and windings from electric motors, and these were surreptitiously plugged into the lighting circuit.

Inevitably, this seriously overloaded the circuits, which were protected with flimsy circular fuses of the Edison screw pattern, resembling a disc of cooking foil. When these fuses blew, the solution was to insert a Dutch five-cent piece, an English shilling or a steel washer. This was only a short-term measure, though, as in the end the overheated mains reacted by blowing all the main fuses in the guardroom, where the resulting minor explosion showered the dozing guards with molten metal (the fuse box was in their sleeping quarters). Next morning everyone was detailed to parade outside our huts while a massive search was made to ascertain the cause of the electrical fault. Naturally, all our illegal appliances were well and truly hidden beforehand, and all that was discovered was a few coins doubling up as fuse discs. These were promptly replaced by the searchers who retired mystified as to the cause of the fuse box fire. After this, we had to be more cautious about overloading the circuits and staggered our nightly cooking to spread the electrical load.

When certain building materials within the camp were exhausted, we obtained permission to salvage them from abandoned buildings outside. Apart from a native village about a mile away, all other habitations in the area, particularly those formerly occupied by Europeans, were deserted and in a forbidden zone. Equipped with a hand cart and a few tools, we would strip out any useful piping, boards or any other material needed for repairs in camp. At first, we were accompanied by one guard, but it proved to be a boring duty (and extra to main-gate picket), so gradually our escort was dropped, and our party, normally no more than four, was allowed out on our daily expeditions wearing only identification armbands. I suppose the Japs reasoned that escape was virtually impossible; our appearance alone would immediately give us away amongst the indigenous population, who were mostly smaller and darker and had an entirely different gait.

This relaxation provided a golden opportunity to make outside contacts and smuggle medical supplies, news and other essential items into camp in daylight. We had a concealed compartment built into the bottom of our handcart, and considerable quantities of contraband, purchased clandestinely from contacts, were carried into camp this way. The handcart was invariably piled with miscellaneous builders' junk and received only the most cursory check from the guardroom sentry, as it differed little from day to day. On one occasion, our secret was almost blown when a loose board fell off the underside of the cart on the approach road to the camp. With what seemed a loud clatter, two large cartons of quinine tablets fell to the ground, followed by a pack of torch batteries and some radio spares. With great presence of mind the cart-pushers kicked these 'red hot' items into the nearby monsoon drain, and without stopping we continued up to the camp gates. Sweating rather more profusely than usual, we managed to pass the guardroom without comment, as no one had apparently seen the incident. Later that night an intrepid member of the camp squirmed under the wire between guard patrols and retrieved the lost contraband from the mud at the bottom of the drain. After suitable washing, the quinine tablets went to the hospital and the rest to the radio-builders, who more than anyone were responsible for our getting up-to-date news from the outside world to counteract the propaganda the Japanese put out that they were winning every battle they fought.

Over and above camp maintenance, we were often called upon to repair or improve the Japanese quarters. On one memorable occasion, when they wanted some tiling in the guardroom shower, two of us set off to retrieve some from outside camp. (This was not impossible, as the majority of Dutch colonial ceilings were tiled, and it simply meant prising what we needed off the nearest suitable source.) For obvious reasons, at least one of our salvage party was a member of the Field Security Police or similar intelligence personnel, whose job it was to make the necessary outside contacts or glean any news from external sources. My companion was an ex-Guardsman, over six feet tall but blessed with a perpetual grin that gave him a rather inane appearance. Nevertheless, he spoke fluent Malay and had a reasonable grasp of Japanese and was anxious to discover what Japanese naval officers were occupying the nearby Royal Netherlands Yacht Club. No one was visible when we approached this palatial residence, and to my consternation my companion proceeded to lift a large section of the patio tiles with a pick.

The area he attacked was the inset insignia of the Royal Yacht Club, and within minutes a scream of rage shattered the air, and an irate Japanese Naval Officer rushed out brandishing a nasty-looking sword. Although he measured only about five feet two inches, he subjected the tall PoW to a furious tirade meanwhile waving his sword about in menacing swipes just missing my companion, who knew that if he stood his ground and did not cower he would probably survive the onslaught. Still grinning inanely, my companion said without changing expression:

'Tell him I'm mad.'

With a mixture of pidgin English and Malay, and the well-known gesture of screwing one finger into the temple, I finally managed to convince the fuming Jap that my partner was a 'screwball'. Curiously enough, and to my relief, he backed off, though not without dire threats that our conduct would be reported back at camp. (We discovered later that most Japanese had a healthy respect for the insane and usually avoided contact with them like the plague, so we were able successfully to use this ruse again.)

When we got back to camp, we finished tiling the guardroom shower, taking care to report our encounter with the naval officer in case of repercussions. But there was little love lost between the Nippon Army and Navy, and our guards thought it a great joke to be showering on their Navy's property. We heard no more of the episode, and our camp intelligence benefited by my companion's close observation of the naval officer's insignia, which confirmed reports we had already gleaned of coastal patrols in our area.

CHAPTER 8
Out and About

Working parties became smaller but more varied and more frequent, so the numbers of prisoners required remained the same. For some of the more distant tasks, it was obvious, even to the Japs, that we would be unfit for work if we had to march all the way there and back. Trucks were therefore provided, although they were not luxurious (most were decrepit, patched-up apologies for transport, unfit for despatch to the battle areas).

Such was the shortage of wheels and tyres that most 30cwt and 3-ton lorries were stripped of one pair of the twin sets of rear wheels normally fitted. The tyres were frequently retreaded crudely by native service stations, and it was common to lose the entire retread during harsh braking on the rough roads. This driving technique seemed to be the norm for Japanese military drivers, who in one week burnt out more clutches and brake linings and stripped more gearboxes than we could achieve in six months of sabotage!

It was the practice to load as many standing PoWs as could be crammed onto each vehicle, which was usually an open truck with stake or batten sides offering little or no protection against falling overboard. Everyone on the outside therefore took the precaution of linking hands and then hoped for the best. On one occasion a truck was driving rapidly along a canal bank when the offside wheels skidded over the edge, and the whole lot lurched into the turgid water. The water broke the PoWs' fall, and, apart from a few bruises and a liberal coating of evil-smelling slime, all scrambled to the bank little the worse. No such luck for the Japanese driver, who was trapped in the cabin under water, presumably having been knocked unconscious.

The second guard, who had been sitting on the cab roof, marshalled us on the canal bank and, after counting us to assure himself no one was missing, prepared to march us off to our destination. At this point a prisoner tactfully pointed out that his mate, the driver, was still trapped in his cab, but the guard merely shrugged his shoulders and brusquely ordered the party to move off, making no attempt to rescue his compatriot. This was one of several instances of Japanese indifference to death and suffering even among their own kind, an attitude that did not bode well for our future treatment.

This particular party, after continuing their journey, found themselves on an airfield where several bomb craters needed filling. During the subsequent clearance of some bomb-damaged hangars a large concrete strong room was discovered with a substantial steel door, securely locked. Oxy-acetylene equipment was procured, and a prisoner with cutting experience was ordered to attack the lock. His efforts were watched by a crowd of expectant Japanese, no doubt visualising a horde of valuables within. The moment the smoking remnants of the lock fell off, the cutting operator was unceremoniously elbowed aside as the Japanese rushed inside – almost as quickly they poured out again in a panic, yelling, 'Aba Nido! Aba Nido!' ('Danger' in Japanese), and made off to the furthest edge of the airfield. The room was full of 500-lb bombs, apparently left by the retreating Dutch Air Force several months before!

Due to the tropical conditions most of these bombs were in a critical condition and 'sweating' their high-explosive contents. Of course, this did not prevent our captors from ordering the bombs to be cleared, and for the next few hours moving them to a safe area was a nail-biting experience for the luckless prisoners, who gingerly manhandled each bomb outside while the guards stayed well out of range of any explosion. Later that evening Japanese engineers detonated the lethal pile behind a large revetment of sandbags.

Another of the miscellaneous chores thrust upon us was clearing the dockside *godowns* (warehouses), many of which had been damaged. The Japanese systematically looted everything of possible value and shipped it away. Food, fuel* and medical supplies went to the distant battle areas of Burma and the southwest Pacific; machinery, scrap metal of all kinds, and any raw

---

* As I have said, fuel oil and aviation spirit were an important part of the cargo of all outgoing convoys. Unlike in Borneo and other Pacific oilfields, where British demolition teams had blown up all the main installations, the Dutch Army had not immobilised Java's and Sumatra's oilfields, and their conquerors soon had them back in almost full production. And failure to deny these facilities to the enemy was only one of the bones of contention we had with our Allies. Whereas the British, Indians, Australians and Americans took great pains to immobilise all abandoned vehicles before surrendering, the Dutch Army inexplicably left many thousands of cars and trucks in roadworthy condition, not even bothering to remove rotor arms. Consequently, the victorious Japanese acquired large numbers of vehicles in pristine condition that were shipped away to be used against the Allies.

materials, were shipped to Japan, whence presumably their facto-
ries returned them later as munitions.

While clearing the *godowns* we seized any opportunity to
smuggle food or medical supplies back to camp. The medical
supplies were often more highly prized than the food (the Japs at
least provided us with an apology for a meal each day, but medical
supplies were non-existent, and our captors were indifferent to
the fact that anyone who died was depleting their work parties).
On occasion, if the Japanese considered the damaged food unsuitable for their own consumption, we would be allowed to carry
considerable quantities back to camp. By this time we had learned
not to be fastidious about what we ate and consequently enjoyed
a variety of foods, from dog biscuits and tinned baby food to
ancient cheese and miscellaneous dry goods which had been
soaked with fire-hoses or contaminated with oil. Our ration scale
in camp was well below European standards, and any addition
to our diet was welcome. Anything edible was tried, even grasses,
leaves and berries, regardless of unpleasant taste. Small wonder
that the majority of prisoners soon succumbed to the combined
effects of continuous hard work and lack of essential vitamins.
And we all lacked salt; there was a general shortage of it in the
tropics even in normal conditions, and in wartime it assumed a
rarity akin to gold dust.

———

In spite of the shortcomings of a prison-camp existence, some
semblance of permanence had become accepted in our daily
routine, particularly as most of the day-to-day working details

became fewer in the Tandjong Priok area. We were almost beginning to accept the fact that we would have to sit it out there for the rest of the war. It was therefore something of a surprise when our captors announced that the camp was to close down and all personnel were to be transferred to Batavia, some fourteen miles inland.

CHAPTER 9
Bicycle Camp

The usual collection of trucks awaited us on the morning of our departure, and to the frenzied shouts of the guards nondescript groups of prisoners were crammed into them like sardines. With some misgivings we prepared to leave our 'home' of the last few months. We were allowed to take with us only what we could carry, and so had to leave behind many 'home comforts'. Those that were too big or too heavy had to be abandoned, together with the various amenities carefully acquired or installed in the camp.

The weak condition of the inmates meant that we took even less than we might normally have expected to carry, and one had to consider which tools, etc., would come in most handy at the next camp. For many of us, this was the first of a series of last-minute moves from one camp to another, and we always had the feeling that the next one was likely to be worse than the one we were leaving: 'better the devil you know, than one you don't!'

During a move the procedure was to carry at least one day's rations in bulk form, as usually none were available when we arrived at a new destination. This was fortunate for our subversive activities, since sacks of rice and beans made excellent hiding places for radio parts, tools and other items likely to be found in the personal searches rigorously carried out at both ends of our journey. Most guards seemed content with a perfunctory stir of the surface of food sacks, though, and in all my camp moves I cannot recall anything so concealed being detected. On this first transfer we came very close, though. A radio had been built into the false bottom of a table drawer belonging to our own senior officer. The Japanese were persuaded that this table was essential to our hospital, and it was conveyed amongst other improvised medical equipment on a separate truck. But when we reached our new camp its Commandant ordered all wooden articles to be piled in the centre of the parade ground and burnt as a disinfestation measure. Although the guardroom overlooked the parade ground, luckily the table was stacked on the side shielded from its view by the rest of the pile, and under cover of darkness one brave lad stole out, retrieved the drawer and silently returned to our billet, where the radio was dismantled and safely dispersed until the time came to reassemble it.

The new camp was something of an improvement on Tandjong Priok and was named 'Bicycle Camp', after the cycle-mounted Dutch colonial troops that had formerly occupied it. The buildings were more substantial single-storey barracks complete with latrines and wash places – comparative luxury after the primitive conditions we had been used to. The one snag was the hopeless overcrowding: some two thousand prisoners were housed in accommodation intended for five hundred peacetime troops. The Japanese Commandant was a rather unpleasant individual called Lt Sonae. The British soon nicknamed him 'Sonny Boy', although he was anything but 'sunny' in his disposition, meting out instant punishment to all and sundry on the least pretext.

He had an oriental unpredictability which never ceased to mystify us. Whether it was an inbuilt inferiority complex driven by his lack of height, or just an aberration of personality that helped him to reach the rank he had, one will never know. Once, while most prisoners were out of camp on work parties, a roving guard entered one of the barrack rooms and removed a valuable wrist-watch from an absent prisoner's belongings. Unknown to the Jap, though, there was a sick prisoner at the far end of the hut who saw the theft and told his pal about it when he returned from the work detail. The owner of the watch promptly reported his loss to the Japanese Commandant – an act of considerable courage, as it was almost unthinkable to accuse a Japanese soldier of stealing. Most commandants would have summarily dismissed the accusation and thrown in a beating-up for good measure, but for some reason Lt Sonae decided to follow it up.

The Japanese, in common with most Orientals, cannot accept a loss of face, and as the British were regarded as the epitome of honesty and fair play, it became a matter of concern to 'Sonny Boy' to remove this slur on his national pride. We did not rate our comrade's chances very high and feared the consequences if the Commandant deemed his accusations unfounded. However, we saw another side of this martinet when he ordered a full parade of all the guards, with the owner of the watch invited to attend. 'Sonny Boy' delivered a harangue to the assembled guards, then in passable English to the PoW by his side he extolled the qualities of honesty and emphasised the dire penalty for false accusation: beheading. After this, the guards were ordered to tip out all their possessions on the parade ground, including all the packs from their quarters.

One has to realise that, according to Japanese military law, bartering with prisoners was strictly forbidden. It was, of course, rife among most guards nonetheless – and, in anticipation of being drafted away shortly, they had also bought clothing and souvenirs in the local town. When the Commandant's gaze fell upon the motley array of 'non-military' items disgorged by his men, his rage knew no bounds. This, we could see, was going to be fun to watch, just so long as our prisoner's watch could be found. Taking the prisoner by the arm 'Sonny Boy' moved slowly along the assembled ranks from one soldier to another, picking up several watches en route. At each soldier he would stop and ask the PoW whether he recognised his own watch. If the answer was 'No', 'Sonny Boy' would ceremoniously dash the watch to the ground and stamp on it, to the consternation of the soldier in question (who, nevertheless, very wisely maintained a rigid, expressionless stance throughout the performance). Inevitably, the missing watch was discovered and, amazingly, returned to the relieved PoW.

The guards were then ordered to pick up only their military items of equipment and return to their billets, leaving one hapless comrade standing to attention amid a jumble of discarded items on the tarmac. 'Sonny Boy' then ordered a party of PoW onlookers to remove all these items and return them to their rightful owners: he was assuming that everything in sight had been acquired inside the camp by his guards – though how he imagined that we had obtained some of the souvenirs I cannot imagine. This was something of a bonus for us, as, of course, some items (even legitimate ex-PoW possessions) had been bartered, with the guards, who had usually paid for them in cigarettes.

The furious Commandant subjected the guilty guard to a frenzied attack for letting him down in front of us prisoners of war. After repeatedly beating with a heavy scabbarded sword the unfortunate victim collapsed and was dragged off to the guard-room, where he was revived with a bucket of cold water and made to stand to attention in a chalk circle 'Sonny Boy' drew in front of the entrance. All guards passing in or out were ordered to strike him with fist or rifle butt: an ordeal which went on throughout the night. Every time the offender collapsed, he was revived with another bucket of water and the process resumed. In the morning the bedraggled figure in front of the guardroom was in a terrible state and was finally dragged off to spend a week in a windowless punishment cell, six feet long and three feet high. He received no medical attention, his daily ration consisted of a small cup of weak tea and one rice ball, and he was offered no exercise or washing facilities. Next he was placed on 48 hours guard duty without relief before a final beating from his CO. Then he was posted to an active service battalion, along with his inevitable broken ribs. Rough justice indeed, and an all-too-clear illustration of the type of captor we were up against – they could be every bit as ruthless to their own kind as they were to us.

Constant working parties and resulting lack of spare time, coupled with the overcrowded conditions, made such activities as radio construction impossible. There was a working radio in the British section of this camp, but imparting any news was made doubly dangerous by the presence of so many prisoners of other nationalities whose silence and security we could not trust. Even in the more established camps where radios functioned, the operation was, for security reasons, confined to a very limited circle, and no news was released until at least a week after it had been received.

It is hard to imagine why some of the prisoners became informants for the Japs, because they were usually treated no differently to the rest of us, having to endure the same food and lack of facilities. They were often in no position to barter a better position for themselves and were discarded by the Japanese at the first opportunity. They would be moved on to other camps and have to suffer the same work parties as the rest of us, but still some continued the practice of giving their comrades away. Those who survived the war were undoubtedly shown little mercy by those they had betrayed.

An example of the mercilessness of the Japanese to one of our prisoner comrades occurred one night when the camp was emptied of Dutch, Indonesian and Indian prisoners who were to leave on draft from Tandjong Priok docks the following morning. A party of British PoWs accompanied them to help with the escorting guards' baggage and distribute some items of shoes and clothing. Each of the draftees assembled on the dockside received a gaily coloured pair of cotton shorts and a cheap pair of plimsolls, described as 'extra clothing comforts' for their journey to Singapore.

One Dutch infantryman was taken with a sudden attack of dysentery, and the Japanese medical corporal ordered him to leave the draft and await transport back to camp. Since he obviously was not joining the embarkation party, he gave his recently acquired plimsolls and shorts to a friend still standing on the dockside. This innocent and generous gesture had dire repercussions when the Japanese sergeant in charge found the friend had two pairs of shorts and plimsolls when he should have had only one. In spite of all his attempts to explain, he was accused of stealing Nippon Army property and beaten to the ground by the irate sergeant, who then proceeded to jump up and down on the hapless Dutchman's inert body. The sheer ferocity of this attack broke his arm and several ribs, one of which punctured his lung. Ignoring all pleas from a Dutch medical officer to remove the injured man to hospital, the brutal sergeant ordered him to be carried on board, and the ship left that night for the mainland and Singapore. There were no medical facilities on board, and, despite superhuman efforts by the Dutch doctor to relieve the poor fellow's suffering, he died next morning and was buried at sea.

CHAPTER 10
Boie Glodok and Tjimahi

Two days later all the British prisoners in Bicycle Camp were marched out to the other side of town to the Boie Glodok gaol, a civil prison that had housed about five hundred native prisoners in peacetime. It was a forbidding place of high walls with lookout towers at the corners and a main entrance gate reminiscent of Dartmoor.

According to the Geneva Conventions, prisoners of war should not have been confined in civil prisons. However, our captors did not recognise this international agreement and considered we had no rights whatsoever, so we had no choice but to accept our lot. The prison cells, ranged each side of long corridors, varied in size and consisted of three bare stone walls fronted by thick steel bars. A small grille opening at high level was the only window, and a tiled hole in one corner represented the sanitary arrangements. Before the Japanese occupation each cell had also had a single water tap in working order, but when we got there no such luxury remained, and water had to be laboriously conveyed every day from the courtyard. Conditions in the cells were uncomfortable to say the least: the floor space averaged around 5 feet by 2 feet per man, and the hard stone flags were no substitute for the makeshift beds we had been used to in our previous camp. The prison buildings enclosed a large court-yard around a hundred yards square with a single open drain running through it. All waste fluid from the cell blocks, guard-room and central kitchen flowed along this drain, through an outer wall and into the nearby river. A team of prisoners had the permanent job of keeping this odious sewage on the move with bamboo scrapers and straw brooms. (A chance meeting with the 'channel sweepers' revealed one of them as the former manager at my local Sainsburys food store; his former employers had been sticklers for hygiene, so he probably felt his knowledge was being put to good use!)

Some of us, notably RAF PoWs, had been interned in this same prison some six months before, when a clandestine radio had been made and buried under the flagstones of a cell. Power came from the existing lighting circuit via concealed wiring, and the operating spindles located in a joint in the stones. When they were transferred to Tandjong Priok camp the cell occupants had to abandon the set and hope it would not be discovered. In fact, although the gaol had later been used by Japanese marines as a barracks, we found the radio intact and still working.

Another radio had come into camp piecemeal and was swiftly brought into operation, but no suitable and convenient hiding place was available, so it was carried around in an old petrol can. The can (doubling as a work tin), along with a towel, was carried into the central ablution block, where there were primitive showers. At suitable broadcast times, usually 9 p.m. at night, a couple of operators would do their daily ablutions, one acting as a lookout for roving sentries. Once, a second, undetected guard almost surprised them, and the operator barely had time to put the set back into its can before strolling nonchalantly out past him. Unknown to the prisoner, in his haste he had left a foot or so of flex dangling outside the tin, but with considerable presence of mind his companion threw his towel over it and diverted the sentries' attention by whistling 'There's a long, long trail a-winding'. The operator got the message, the whistler got a cuff round the head from the guard – the Japanese could not stand whistlers (as I discovered, being an inveterate whistler myself) – and the radio was spirited away to safety.

Radios were our only reliable source of news, and in spite of frequent searches very few were ever discovered by our captors. When they were, the consequences did not bear thinking about, and in retrospect I shudder at what happened to some PoWs found in possession of, or in the process of constructing, a receiver. After a severe beating would come the inevitable inter-rogation and prolonged torture, interspersed with periods of solitary confinement in appalling conditions. No operator who fell into the clutches of the Kempetai, the Japanese Secret Police, ever survived their inhumane treatment: if they did not die as a result of the mental and physical torture, their tormentors sentenced them to death by beheading or bayoneting, or simply shot them.

——————

The Japanese punished even minor infringements severely, including trying to buy or barter food from the natives. One pris-oner, caught exchanging a leather wallet for some bananas with a native, was beaten up by two guards and thrown into solitary confinement. The Indonesian vendor was tied to a tree outside the main gate of the prison with barbed wire and left in the blazing sun, with food and water placed on the ground out of his reach. Every work party entering and leaving the prison, including passing natives, sympathised with the poor wretched man, who became delirious with heat and pain after three days without food or water. He received no medical attention, only daily taunts from the guards, who often kicked and punched him as they passed. On the fourth day, mercifully, he died, but his limp body was left for several days more as a warning, before was cut down and carried away.

Meanwhile, in his solitary confinement, the PoW involved was being systematically starved by the Japanese, who reduced his ration to one small dish of cold rice a day and one cup of water. No arrangements were made for washing or tending his many cuts and bruises, and his cell – none too clean on his arrival – became progressively filthier. During the night someone contrived to slip a banana and a hard-boiled egg through the bars, which he promptly devoured. Such was his hunger that the banana skin was consumed as well, but the eggshell was his undoing. An observant guard noticed the fresh fragments in the general filth on the cell floor, and uproar ensued. The entire prison population was called on parade to hear a diatribe from the Commandant about the evils of passing food to a man on sentence. The subsequent order for the guilty person to own up evoked no response.

The Commandant then issued the ultimatum that, if no one confessed, the entire parade 'would stand to attention until further notice, without food, water or medical attention, come rain, wind or sun until all men die!' Naturally, no one came forward, and a battle of wills began. The ordeal lasted the rest of a blistering hot day and well into the night. A heavy machine-gun was brought out and trained on our assembled ranks, who were encouraged to stand stock still by roving guards who beat anyone making the slightest movement. Towards nightfall many of the weaker men had collapsed, but no one was allowed to attend to them, and they lay where they had fallen. No one was permitted to visit the latrines, and several dysentery cases were in a parlous state, unable to control their bodily functions. Around midnight the infuriated Commandant, having received no response from our ranks, ordered his guards to drag the bed-ridden patients from the camp sick bay and place them on the ground in front of us.

At this stage a young RAF officer bravely stood forward and accepted the blame for passing the illicit food to the PoW in solitary. He was marched off to the guardroom, and the parade was dismissed. Then another inexplicable feature of the Japanese character manifested itself. We fully expected the young officer to receive a severe beating at the least, but the Commandant seemed to realise that, as an officer, he was shouldering the blame for someone else, and he actually complimented him on doing so. A nominal sentence of seven days in the cooler was awarded, after which the officer returned to the main camp to the acclamation of us all.

The two main tasks during our stay in Glodok concerned sisal and salvage. Sisal work – restricted to those too sick to accompany the outside work parties – involved the soul-destroying chore of using primitive hand looms to make sisal string, which was then woven into rice bags and ropes (and the sisal fibres caused painful cuts to the hands that, due to lack of vitamins, rarely healed completely). There was a large motor works in Batavia, formerly American-owned, where most of the salvaged vehicles were eventually dismantled and cannibalised for spare parts. Daily work parties laboured at this depot, mainly assembling and dispatching truck engines destined for Japanese army vehicles in the field. But by now, things were not going too well for the enemy in the Pacific area, and efforts redoubled to collect scrap metal to feed the homeland foundries. Supply convoys were now under constant attack from Allied submarines and long-range aircraft, and raw materials were consequently in short supply, so parties of prisoners and their guards were detailed to visit premises all over Batavia to strip out everything that could usefully be salvaged. Machinery, piping, toilet cisterns, sewing machines, stoves, refrigerators, railings and street lamps – all were commandeered and loaded onto lorries en route for the docks. Many items were taken from occupied premises, to the loud protests of the unfortunate owners and occupants. The era of prosperity and abundance the victorious Japanese had promised the locals was now ringing rather hollow!

One day, though, with typical lack of warning, these activities abruptly ceased, and we were marched back to Bicycle Camp again, where we heard that all fit men would form the basis of the next draft. An unprecedented series of crude medical checks was carried out by teams of Japanese in white coats and face masks, accompanied by some stolid-faced nurses (none of whom, despite the absence of female company for over twelve months, stirred even the faintest sexual feelings among us). The upshot was that the enemy finally realised none of us were in the least bit fit, certainly not strong enough for a long sea voyage. They decided to send us to a healthier camp in the foothills of Java, where sulphur springs abounded and where they fondly hoped our condition would improve and permit our early despatch overseas. Within a week we were on the move again, entrained for Tjimahi, a large camp near central Java.

Tjimahi had formerly been one of the largest barracks in the Dutch East Indies and was close to an airfield. The buildings were more European, being roomy and clean – although, as we shared them with several thousand captured Dutch and Indonesian troops, there was still a considerable overcrowding problem. Our diet improved somewhat, now being augmented by vegetables and spices from the prolific plot that had been part of the original barracks kitchen gardens. A permanent piped water supply and bath houses dispensing hot sulphurous water from underground springs was much better than our previous sparse washing facilities and considerably alleviated the multitude of skin complaints we all suffered from. All the same, it wasn't quite the 'rest cure' the Japanese promised; there was a thriving sisal operation, and we had to make our quota of rice bags or sisal mats while 'convalescing'.

Every day six prisoners would be detailed to accompany the ration truck and help with loading and unloading rice and other food from nearby Bandung. Once, returning to camp at the usual breakneck speed, the Jap driver misjudged the gate opening and overturned the truck. The PoWs were thrown onto a grass verge and suffered nothing worse than a few bruises, but the driver collected a broken arm, cracked ribs and a gashed forehead. The irate guard commander had this unfortunate hauled before him to receive a blistering tirade, which lasted over half an hour before the injured fellow collapsed. Then the guard commander ordered him to be carried away, but only to reappear later, heavily bandaged and with one arm in a sling, to be placed on twelve hours' guard duty as a punishment.

Some of us had the less demanding chore of caring for the teams of horses used by a local detachment of Japanese artillery. Their field pieces were 18-pounders of World War I vintage, formerly used by the Dutch East Indies Army, and the horses were mainly of Australian stock. Our first encounter with the horses was rather unpleasant, as they tended to kick out and bare their teeth. This, we discovered, was their natural reaction to the cruel treatment of their new masters, and indeed the Japanese artillerymen were afraid to go too near them. Like most animals, these horses soon learned to distinguish those who treated them kindly from those who did not, and we soon made some friends and allies among them. The Japanese they hated most was the regimental 'blacksmith' – the merest amateur at shoeing horses. One day he met his match, when one of the larger draught horses reacted to an ill-placed nail with an almighty kick that lifted the man off the ground and flung him a full twenty feet; he died later that day from internal injuries.

John Baxter, photographed in March 1941 shortly after he was conscripted.

Men of the 77th HAA/RA disembarking from the *Warwick Castle* at Batavia
(now Jakarta) in February 1942. Less than 24 hours later they were involved
in a train crash which killed 26 men and left many more crippled for life.

John Baxter
photographed in
Java in March 1942.

John Baxter's
bed-tag at Bogor
'hospital', 1942.

INTERNATIONAL RED CROSS COMMITTEE DELEGATE

TOKYO, JAPAN

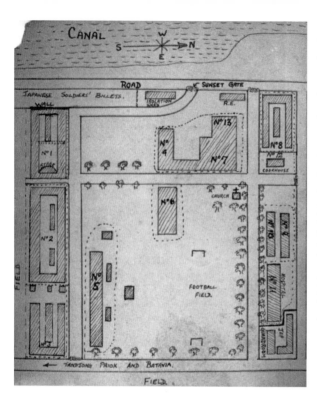

A plan of the 'Uniekampong', the PoW camp at Tandjong Priok, Java, where the author was held between 1942 and 1943. The plan was drawn by Captain A.A. Duncan of the Argyll & Scottish Highlanders, while he was imprisoned at the camp between March and October 1942. Reproduced by kind permission of Meg Parkes, Captain Duncan's daughter.

The only known photograph of St George's chapel, Tandjong Priok. It was taken by the Japanese on 12 July 1942 for propaganda purposes and appeared a year later in an article in the *Nippon Times* dated 27 June 1943. The picture shows the Service of Consecration of the Chapel. The author is third from the left.

John Baxter's identity tag and prisoner number whilst he was held at Camp 8, Kamoo, Fukuoka, Japan, 1943–45.

The Lancashire Boiler Detail (Kamoo 1944) J. Baxter

Using a sled, crowbars and a primitive winch, PoWs from Camp 8 transport a Lancashire-built boiler two miles from the railway depot to the pithead boiler-house.

Christmas 1943 at Camp 8. The author is holding an empty bottle!

Tenko (meaning 'roll call') parade at Camp 8. The author is on the left of the picture, in the second row, wearing a peaked cap.

Survivors of Camp 8, photographed in August 1945 shortly after the Japanese surrender. The author is sitting on the ground, third from the right.

The author and his wife Lilian (left) with Lady Mountbatten in the village of Papworth Everard, Cambridgeshire, in the early 1950s.

John Baxter (right) with his son, also called John, and his former guard Hirano, in Fukuoka, Japan, 1995.

John Baxter photographed with his granddaughter Charlotte in 2009 on his 90th birthday. The picture was taken in Holy Trinity Church, Trowbridge, Wiltshire.

Tjimahi camp was one of the better camps in Java for food and accommodation, and our health improved marginally because it was located above the mosquito-ridden lowlands. But we suffered from a particularly mean crowd of Japanese and, for the first time, some of their Korean conscripts. We soon learned to our discomfort that there was little love lost between the Koreans and their masters, and consequently we frequently felt the butt of the Koreans' sense of inferiority. They could be far nastier than the Japanese at times.

Shortly before we arrived at Tjimahi, several Dutch escapees had been shot before a full parade of prisoners, and feelings on both sides were running high. In an attempt to defuse the situation the Japanese decided on a 'presento' parade to coincide with the Emperor's birthday. All prisoners were given a day's holiday and paraded in the main square to be presented with a minute satsuma as a gesture of Nippon's benevolence.

We were rapidly devouring these in case they changed their minds and took them away when a flypast of gleaming Mitsubishi bombers from the local airfield slowly roared over, probably to impress us with the 'superior' might of the glorious Nippon Air Force. Unfortunately, a captured US Martin bomber was being flight tested from another nearby airfield, and its crew obviously knew nothing about the special flypast. The Martin had hardly become airborne when it collided head-on with the first echelon, and a mid-air explosion wrote off two new bombers. This rather dampened the day's festivities, and the screaming guards rushed everyone back into the billets.

For the rest of our stay at Tjimahi relations were distinctly strained, and it was a relief when we were moved back to Batavia, to the Bicycle Camp again. But we were only there for nine days. There was another farcical medical inspection and, wonder of wonders, we were issued with clothing: our first since the beginning of captivity. This consisted of one gaudy pair of striped shorts, one pair of second-hand Japanese army rubber shoes, and a second-hand Dutch army jacket. Most of the items were intended for Asiatics, who were considerably smaller than the average Briton – but beggars could not be choosers, and we added them to our sparse kit with a view to future modification.

It must be remembered that we had now spent some eighteen months of captivity in Java without receiving Red Cross supplies of any description, although a rare one or two letters had miraculously reached some fortunate PoWs (goodness only knows how). In spite of constant representation by our own officers, the Japanese made little attempt to forward details of prisoners to a neutral power. Consequently, little was known of our whereabouts back home, where most of us had been posted as 'missing, believed killed or prisoner'. Our one and only opportunity to write a letter came after we had been in captivity over six months. This took the form of a single sheet of rice paper about 10 in × 8 in, on which our captors instructed us to stress that we were all well and being cared for in good camps. All these heartfelt messages were promptly collected and laboriously read by the Jap interpreter before (as we later learned) being consigned to the nearest bonfire.

On 10 September 1943, our ninth day in Bicycle Camp, some five hundred of us were finally pronounced fit enough to travel. We packed our few worldly possessions and marched out to Tandjong Priok docks for the first stage of the most momentous journey we were to undertake in the next two years.

CHAPTER 11
Singapore and Points East

Like dozens of previous drafts, we assembled on the humid dockside at Tandjong Priok where we had spent many a back-breaking hour in recent months, and nervously eyed the ship that was to transport us. It was a battered old island coaster of almost 3000 tons named the *Van Waerwijk*. She had originally been scuttled in Priok harbour by the Dutch; then, after several unsuccessful attempts, the rusting hulk had been salvaged by the Japanese and was now pressed into service as the *Harukiku Maru* between Java and Singapore. As we filed aboard, it was evident that the holds were already full of miscellaneous cargo, and our party of five hundred was dispersed about the decks in the open air. Some were more fortunate than others, securing cover in cattle pens secured to the well deck, but the remainder were exposed to the elements. Within minutes of the last man coming aboard, the ship cast off and, with an asthmatic wheezing of the engines, made for the open sea.

The cool sea breezes were a welcome change from the oppressive humidity of the mainland, and we settled down as best we could. The ship was heavy-laden and had less than two feet of freeboard, rolling heavily even in the slightest swell. Several pumps clanked noisily, keeping pace with numerous leaks, and we mistrusted our chances in a storm. No such luxuries as lifebelts were visible, and the sole lifeboat was obviously intended for the crew, which gave us even more cause for concern.

By now we knew from our clandestine radios that Allied submarines were in the area and had caused great loss to several previous convoys. Since the Japanese did not mark ships carrying prisoners of war or notify the Red Cross of human shipments, we ran a considerable risk of being sunk by our own side. Indeed we later learned that many thousands of PoWs lost their lives this way, unable to free themselves from the holds of torpedoed or bombed ships – and even those able to swim clear could not expect to be picked up by the Japanese, so most perished from drowning, exposure or shark attack. It was some consolation, therefore, to note that we were hugging the shores of Java and Sumatra and hopping from island to island through the archipelago as we approached Malaya.

During the day we often had air cover from Japanese bases, but at night the ship usually anchored close inshore. En route we passed Bangka Island, where the Japanese had restored the high-pressure hydraulic tin-mining monitors: powerful water jets that simply washed away the overburden and disclosed the veins of ore. The massive erosion of the coastal belt was evident from miles of yellow discoloration in the sea approaches to Bangka.

Luckily the weather stayed fine for this short voyage, although the typhoon season was imminent. In spite of the lack of cover on deck, we managed to keep cool with the breeze of the ship's movement and frequent washing with a solitary sea-water hose. Food was not too much of a problem, as a plentiful supply of coarse rice and sea food was cooked twice daily on deck in charcoal braziers. Even the escorting guards did nothing to disturb us and seemingly treated this 'cruise' as a welcome break from their otherwise strict discipline.

The third day after leaving Java we docked in Singapore and disembarked to find a convoy of trucks awaiting us. These were driven by renegade Indian PoWs who had elected to join the Japanese-aligned Indian National Army instead of entering captivity. (We subsequently learnt that some of these men had told other prisoners they were only awaiting a suitable opportunity to escape back to India, but we were not so sure and treated them with much caution in case they were trying to spy on our activities for the Japanese.) When the trucks were full, the convoy sped off at breakneck speed through the teeming streets to the infamous Changi gaol on the other side of Singapore Island.

The pre-war British administration had also built the main army barracks near the prison, and at one time over 80,000 prisoners of war were housed in the surrounding encampments. Our party was allocated to some long wooden huts that had been occupied in peacetime by Indian Army personnel. As soon as contact could be made with the locally based prisoners of war news was eagerly exchanged and friendships renewed with some who had arrived at Singapore from previous drafts. We learned that the first-ever shipment of Red Cross supplies had arrived in Malaya a few weeks before – South African clothes, medical supplies and a limited amount of mail. Unfortunately, there wasn't enough for everyone, and our party did not qualify for anything other than a few dozen letters (for many, the first since capture over eighteen months earlier). I was one of the lucky ones, receiving a heavily censored forces air letter from an old workmate serving in the Middle East. In it he managed to convey that he had surmised that I might be a prisoner and promised to notify my parents that he had a forwarding address (i.e. Singapore) where it was thought I would ultimately pass through.

While we were in Changi we learned of the terrible conditions on the mainland of Malaya and Burma, with the construction of the infamous 'Railway of Death'. Literally dozens of parties of Allied prisoners had been sent up-country from Singapore to what the Japanese officially and euphemistically described as a 'rest camp'. All preceding drafts from Java and Sumatra had been summarily despatched to Burma, regardless of physical condition, the promise of 'good food and medical attention' being offered by our captors as an incentive and to prevent officers from arguing that the sick should be allowed to stay in Singapore. Initially, it looked as if we were to form the next railway party – as most were in batches of 500, which happened to be the size of our contingent. However, there seemed to be no immediate need, for we were first detailed on various local chores.

Our two principal tasks were logging parties and airfield construction. The first was essential, as fuel was in very short supply, and timber was exclusively used to fire the cookhouse stoves. We would march off to the nearest rubber plantations – which, curiously enough, had been left unattended by the Japanese – and were ordered to systematically cut down dozens of otherwise healthy trees for firewood. These would be loaded onto trailers made from the stripped chassis of old army trucks and towed by manpower back to the log piles at the camp.

This was a comparatively healthy occupation compared to

building the airfield at Kranji. This was surrounded by the most evil-smelling swampland one can imagine, and hundreds of half-naked PoWs were made to move tons of rubble and coral rocks by hand to fill it in and extend the runway. Men would be wading knee deep in slimy water before dumping their load at the spot designated by the Jap engineer in charge. Every splash caused by the lumps of hardcore or human movement in the turgid water would release clouds of voracious mosquitoes, not to mention dozens of tiny leeches that festooned themselves around one's calves. We were forbidden to smoke while working, which would have given us the chance to burn off the leeches, and the general shortage of oil prevented the Japanese from spraying the area. Thus every day was a seemingly endless and frustrating torment that only ceased when we got back to Changi, where we could expect the luxury of a cold shower and have our daily wounds inspected.

After a week of this, we were interviewed by an English-speaking Japanese of uncharacteristically pleasant disposition, who told us our party had been selected to go to Japan.

'You will find conditions much more civilised and comfort-able,' he assured us. 'You will, of course, be housed in European-style camps and have access to ample Red Cross supplies. Everyone will be allowed to write home regularly and encouraged to undertake light work in order to keep fit in prepa-ration for the day we return home to our friends and families.'

We had the feeling that this tale had been regurgitated many times before, so we took it with a shovelful of salt. However, given the terrible reports coming from up-country, we were thankful it was not to be the dreaded Burma Railway detail, and we set to, yet again, to pack up for the next move. The same surly group of Indian drivers collected us and returned us to Singapore docks, where a large convoy was apparently assembling for return to Japan. At the dockside a large ship was berthed, and amid the turmoil of loading activity, we walked up the gang plank to begin yet another journey into the unknown.

The ship was the *Ussuri Maru*, a passenger ship built on the Clyde and operated in the Pacific during the depression of the 1930s. A four-deck superstructure gave her a top-heavy look, and we referred to her as 'Queen Anne's Mansions'. The lower decks were crammed with 500 Japanese artillerymen and, above them, a number of civilian VIPs and technicians returning home. The well decks were full of captured Bofors anti-aircraft guns which, with their gunners, were en route to bolster the homeland air defences. Otherwise, the only defensive armament on board was an antiquated 18-pounder field gun mounted in the bows and surrounded by sandbags.

Every available space not used for essential access was filled with cargo of all descriptions – crates, drums and bulk packages, lashed down ready for sea. The lower hold was full of bauxite, and we PoWs were quartered in the upper hold in the aft part of the ship. The bauxite was covered with tarpaulins, but this did not stop its red dust from permeating every nook and cranny of our quarters, and we soon got used to being permanently coated in it. Some rough wooden bunks ringed the hold, and we soon discovered a pile of tattered life jackets evidently left by former Japanese Army occupants.

The next day, 20 September 1943, the *Ussuri Maru* cast off and manoeuvred into Singapore Bay to join the assembled shipping awaiting its escorts. The convoy appeared to consist of several tankers and a number of other ships loaded to the gunwales with deck cargoes. Finally we steamed off in a tropical downpour: 32 ships in all, escorted by two destroyers and a lone aircraft flying slowly back and forth until overtaken by night.

Everyone felt this was likely to be our most hazardous journey yet; Japan had been suffering even more reverses at sea, and few if any convoys in the Pacific area reached their destinations unscathed. We would have to run the gauntlet of Allied submarines now becoming very active, and later might suffer the attentions of land-based Allied aircraft operating from China. Not a happy thought, particularly as we were not only the largest vessel in the convoy, but also the heaviest-laden – and totally unmarked to denote the presence of PoWs.

Conditions below deck, somewhat claustrophobic, were made just about tolerable by our being allowed on deck once a day in batches to use a deck latrine and to cool off with a small sea-water hose. Food was limited to two meals a day of boiled rice with a minute portion of dried fish or radish. The only liquid was about a pint of weak tea – no milk or sugar, of course. A shortage of fresh water meant we could not shave, even with our blunt razors, so we all began to grow fearsome-looking beards. Shortly after settling below deck, we discovered a store of pickled vegetables in casks, and this supplemented our diet for the remainder of the voyage – even vinegar can taste special after a while! Due to the laxity of our guards, the loss was not discovered during our occupancy of the hold, and the empty cases were secreted in the loose depths of the bauxite cargo.

When we were out of range of air cover, the convoy adopted a procedure that entailed hugging friendly coastline where practicable, interspersed by short dashes across open sea between the major islands. Unknown to us, our progress was being constantly monitored by the Allies, and a reception party of a pack of US submarines was being arranged for the approaches to the Philippines.

About seven days out of Singapore, we were taking our daily one-hour stroll on deck, drying off after a hose-down, when one of us spotted the wake of a torpedo heading obliquely towards us. Fortunately for us, the *Ussuri Maru* was in the throes of completing a zigzag pattern, part of the usual convoy evasive action, blissfully unaware of the destruction that was about to occur. As our ship and the one to starboard turned in unison, the latter's bows cut across the torpedo's path. That ship had no chance at all. A thunderous explosion blew her bows completely off, flinging a gun and its crew a good 150 feet in the air, and seconds later the ship erupted in a massive blast of flame, as the deck cargo of aviation fuel exploded. She was still ploughing ahead at full speed and literally slid straight under the surface in less than five minutes, leaving a patch of blazing fuel punctuated with spouts of steam as the only evidence of its departure. There were no survivors.

All hell then broke loose in the convoy as the panic-stricken Japs blasted off into the sky with every gun available. It was clear from their reactions that only we had seen the torpedo at first, and our captors thought that the sunken vessel had been either bombed or shelled. We watched all this with some excitement but were soon unceremoniously bundled below, and thereafter could only surmise how things were progressing up top.

Meanwhile the *Ussuri Maru* had speeded up and was taking progressively more violent evasive action, which resulted in a very rough passage for the succeeding hours. Muffled explosions at frequent intervals indicated that the Japs had now realised submarines were involved, and so were dropping depth charges. It is awe-inspiring to be in the bowels of a speeding ship in a rough sea and feel the concussion of underwater explosions hitting its steel sides. The more experienced sailors amongst us could distinguish between the explosion of a depth charge and a torpedo hit, and it became ominously evident that the convoy was suffering considerable losses. Miraculously, we were still proceeding unscathed, probably because we were one of the faster ships in the convoy. Also, the weather was worsening, and it became clear, that our Japanese captain was deliberately heading for the typhoon area to try and shake off his pursuers. We prayed our British-built ship would stay the course.

Night fell, and we were still ploughing fast through heavy seas, distant explosions reminding us that we were not yet clear of danger. Later the wind increased, the waves became mountainous, and our voyage rapidly became an ordeal we would all remember for years. For days and nights the storm battered us without respite, and we struggled on, the heavily loaded ship shuddering violently and tortured plating creaking and groaning as hundreds of tons of sea water crashed down on the decks. At least the submarines had disappeared, but we were now concerned about our own safety from the ferocious elements

Everything had been battened down below decks including our party of PoWs, and the shriek of tangled metal as objects were literally torn from the decks above us was frightening in the extreme. Conditions were becoming untenable because of the lack of fresh air and toilet facilities, but there was no alternative except to endure until the ship had ridden out the worst of the weather. Somehow the cooks managed to produce some food and hot tea, but visits to the on-deck latrines or any kind of washing was out of the question. The latrine problem was simply solved by emptying the sanitary buckets into the sandy depths of the bauxite cargo, but this did nothing to improve the foetid atmosphere created by hundreds of unwashed bodies in the poorly ventilated cargo decks. I tried to console myself by remarking to my comrades that 'Somewhere there is always someone worse off than ourselves', but this gave us little comfort, as nobody could suggest who that someone might be or how their journey could be worse than ours!

We were immensely relieved when the ship limped into Manila in the Philippines after five of the most uncomfortable days I had spent since capture. An exhausted and dishevelled crowd of prisoners was allowed on deck to breathe some fresh air and take a turn at the sea-water hose. But the sight that met our eyes was proof of the pounding we had received. The decks were a mass of twisted metal and splintered woodwork, and the deck latrines had been washed overboard, together with two lifeboats and several of the Bofors guns that had been lashed together. We also learned that two sentries had been lost when a tremendous wave wrenched off the side rail to which their life-line was attached. Repairs were put in hand while we were anchored in Manila Bay. Over the next day or two the remnants of our convoy made their appearance. Of the original convoy of 32 vessels, only we and four other ships had survived, and we regarded ourselves as extremely fortunate.*

Our route to Japan still entailed steaming through some hazardous waters, and the crew was rather jittery and irritable when the ship finally completed repairs and departed for Taiwan, our next port of call. However, we got there without incident and docked for a day to take on water and fuel. Then, with the benefit of air cover from a large flying boat, we threaded our way gingerly through the chain of islands south of Japan. It was late October when, after a miserable and frightening five weeks at sea, we finally berthed at Moji (now part of the city of Kitakyushu), a large port in the north of Kyushu Island, southern Japan.

---

* There was a sequel to this many years later. In the early 1980s my local Anglican church in Trowbridge entertained a party of a dozen or so Presbyterians from the USA for a fortnight, and I offered to act as guide to the various places in the West Country we took them to during their stay. At one of the parties we held for them I got chatting to a man of around my age. He asked where I had been based in World War II, and I told him some of my experiences. Listening to my account of this attack by Allied submarines he fell silent; then he told me he had been a submarine commander in the Pacific. When I mentioned the date of the attack he could hardly believe his ears. 'I was in charge of that attack on that convoy on that day!' he said. 'We only heard later that many of the boats were carrying PoWs and, unknown to us, a number of the boats we sent to the bottom had been packed to the gunwales with innocent men'.

CHAPTER 12
Japan

We reached Moji at night, and all prisoners were disembarked and housed in a large dockside building pending arrangements for our journey inland. The temperature had dropped considerably, the building was unheated, and we still wore our flimsy tropical rags, so we spent a miserable and uncomfortable time huddled together for warmth. Typically, no food had been issued since our last meal aboard the *Ussuri Maru*, some rice and tea at midday the previous day, so we were cold, hungry and dishevelled when we assembled in the early hours of the next morning to march to the railway station.

The drab streets of Moji were depressing. Throngs of youths, old men and women were on their way to work, dressed in patched, shapeless clothing that would not have looked out of place on a prisoner of war. Recognising us as the hated enemy, they jeered and gesticulated as we passed, but guttural shouts from our guards made them keep their distance. This, then, was the legendary Japan where we had been promised a better existence and treatment on European terms. We hoped this introduction was not a foretaste of things to come, but we felt very pessimistic about our prospects.

When we reached the station, our party of five hundred was divided into two contingents, each going to a separate destination. Meanwhile, we were given our first meal on Japanese soil: a *bento* – a small wooden box about eight inches long, five inches wide and two inches deep. This one contained a portion of cold cooked rice and a thin slice of *daikon*, a kind of radish. (We were to discover that *bento* was a universal term for a packed ration of this kind, used by all and sundry to this day.) Our first and only experience of comfortable travel, Japanese-style, arrived in the shape of fairly modern, commuter-style railway carriages, complete with flush-type toilets. These were the most modern we encountered during our captivity – but we quickly discovered they were used by either sex. Later that afternoon, the train arrived in the foothills of a mountain range in Fukuoka Prefecture, one of the sub-divisions of Kyushu Island. We had not seen much of the countryside (the blinds had been drawn by our guards), and it was a curious bunch of PoWs that piled out of the carriages at the small station of Kamoo, which served the nearby village of Inatsuki. We marched off through a large village of wooden houses, the road lined with crazy pine poles supporting power lines. The road was unmetalled, with large potholes and puddles, and groups of grinning locals lined up to jeer us on our way. Soon we came in sight of what were unmistakably pithead workings, and then our future occupation became clear.

On the way to our camp, we passed the local police station, where a Japanese youth was hanging upside down by his feet in the doorway. Our guards told us he was a local thief, and this was part of his punishment: everyone passing through the doorway was required to punch or kick him as he swung there. Thus we discovered that the mediaeval practices we had thought only applied to the military and foreign nationals in the confines of our prison camps affected Japanese civilians as well.

About a mile and a half from the station was the camp, lying in a hollow midway between the village and two large coal mines. The whole area was drab and uninviting; there was hardly a blade of grass or a tree to be seen, and nearby slag heaps and the distant mountain were the only relief in an almost featureless view. This was an anti-climax after the vistas of greens and other colours in the tropics and, coupled with the cold, damp atmosphere, implied rather a depressing outlook for the future. The camp was quite small, about two hundred yards square, and consisted of long wooden huts around an earth compound. The site was enclosed by a high wooden fence topped by strands of electrified barbed wire and overlooked by a guardroom at the top of a long earthen ramp.

The huts were built Japanese-style of light weatherboarding with felt roofs and raised internal floors with straw mats, known as *tatami*s. The windows were lightweight wooden frames with rice paper stuck on, sliding in grooved channels attached to the outer walls. The rooms were about 12 feet square, so, with six men allocated to each, this averaged 48 men per hut. A single electric light bulb illuminated each compartment, but there was no switch, and the power was controlled from the guardroom. Until air raids became more frequent, these lights were kept on all night, and we had to suffer this inconvenience when trying to sleep. The huts were not heated, and our 'hosts' told us that the winters could be very cold, so each man received an issue of threadbare blankets and (wonder of wonders!) a stone hot-water bottle. Sadly, few of these bottles survived the first winter; they were so poorly made that most cracked the first time they were filled with hot water.

One of the huts was a communal bath-house, so we all rapidly had our first hot bath for over eighteen months. The bath-house consisted of a large sunken concrete tank, about twelve feet square and three feet deep with a batten floor, under which a coil of heating pipe rested. This was heated from a small external boiler, the tending of which soon became one of the more sought-after chores in camp, as it at least ensured that the stoker kept reasonably warm. Cold showers completed the installation and were to provide useful refreshment when one emerged from a well-patronised bath (which got rather turgid after 250 men had used it). At the bottom end of the camp was the mess hut and cookhouse, a building large enough to seat the entire camp. The cookhouse consisted merely of a range of cast iron *kwalis* or over-sized Chinese woks, built like old-fashioned British coppers on brick bases with a fireplace underneath. No other equipment was provided except for some ladles and wooden pails, and every-thing we subsequently ate was prepared in these *kwalis*.

The day after our arrival at 'Camp 8, Kamoo', as it was called, the Japanese made their first serious attempt to catalogue the prisoners in their charge.* We were first paraded and ordered to

---

* Hitherto our fate had been something of a mystery back in Britain, for no attempt had been made to compile accurate records, and it was 18 months before the International Red Cross could prise enough infor-mation out of the Nippon government to relay back to Europe. Unfortunately, in the months since our surrender many prisoners had died, and details of their demise were often difficult to trace – especially if they had died at the hands of the vicious Japanese secret police, the Kempetai, who would often have taken them away from the camp for punishment or interrogation.

remove all our hair and the luxurious beards grown during our voyage to Japan. This proved rather painful, as only two pairs of scissors and four blunt cut-throat razors were issued, along with a minute portion of 'ersatz' soap. (After the mass barbering these were carefully checked by the guards and removed.) The finished product was as desperate a bunch of criminal-looking characters as ever graced the portals of Dartmoor Prison!

Heads closely cropped and stubbly chins sporting numerous cuts, we reported, one by one for a civilian photographer to record our glowering countenances, and thereafter a Rogues Gallery of every prisoner, complete with allocated number in Japanese and English, hung in a prominent position in the Commandant's office. For the remainder of our captivity, we were required at all times to carry a tag on which our nationality and number appeared, and (since most Japanese could not pronounce our names) we were always addressed by our number. We were also introduced to a crash course in basic Japanese – including numbers from 1 to 10 and at least a dozen words of command – that had to be mastered in seven days, on pain of instant punishment. Japanese is not the easiest of languages, and during the following weeks we suffered much through various misunderstandings until, through dire necessity or severe beatings from our guards, we mastered the essentials. I was allocated the number 238 (pronounced 'ni-san-hachi').

After the photographic session came an 'assessment' parade which, our captors claimed, provided 'an official record for the Red Cross and to determine our capabilities for suitable interesting work'. It was also a way of getting as much information as possible out of us, and our only British officer, Captain Williams, advised us to give our name, rank, number and the address of our next of kin, but to conceal information on any occupation or experience, civil or military, that might be construed by the Japanese as beneficial to their war effort.

Everyone was again paraded and passed before a Japanese interpreter armed with foolscap questionnaire on which we were expected to declare dozens of details, ranging from the nationality of our grandparents and details of our education, starting with primary school, to details of both civilian and military training in any technical capacity. Needless to say, the most conflicting and derisory data were entered on the questionnaire to confuse our captors, and we needed great self-control to avoid bursting into laughter at the solemn way the interpreter entered these 'gems' of rubbish into his record book. In the faint hope that the recorded information might influence our future work as prisoners, we entered fanciful occupations under 'Trade or Profession'. I tried 'Librarian', but, as we really expected, such answers had no bearing whatever on our destiny, and we were all, without exception, detailed off into shifts for work in the nearby coal mines.

CHAPTER 13
The Mines

The district boasted two large mines, known respectively as Tatako Koni and Kofni with attendant main workshops called Kosako Denki and Kosako Tatako, run by the Mitsui Company. In addition to the mines, a deep shaft was being driven vertically some distance away to try and strike a new seam of coal and eliminate the long hauls currently necessary in the two existing mines, which were becoming increasingly uneconomic to work. Being drift mines, these were approached by long, sloping tunnels into the mountainside, down which trains of trucks were lowered and raised by means of cables from winch houses on the surface. Shifts of miners included Koreans, Japanese and other prisoners besides our party.

We had previously been issued with miners' hats – made of canvas and fibreboard, with a mere half-inch of rubber padding in the crown – and at the pithead electric battery lamps were fixed to them, with the battery box strapped on one's shoulder. Descending groups would then sit in a line of steel trucks fitted with wooden seats before entering the darkness below in a manner that was hair-raising to say the least. The winchman would release his brake, whereupon the whole train of a dozen trucks or so would hurtle at breakneck speed in pitch darkness down a gradient of at least 1 in 10. After what seemed an eternity, but was probably about half a mile, there would be a squeal of tortured metal as the rear brake man applied his retarding wheel, and the clattering trucks would rock to a standstill on the first level section underground. Picks, crowbars and drills were then collected from a store at the drift base, and the party proceeded to the nearest working coal face attended by two or more civilian mine deputies armed with pick-axe handles. The guards did not accompany us underground, and all discipline was enforced by these *hancho*s or Japanese mine foremen, who earned themselves the undying hatred of the British prisoners, by their unrelenting cruelty within the pit.

The mines had been pretty well worked out, with only small seams of pretty low-grade coal remaining, and much of that in solid rock. Consequently it was a long trek from the winding drift to the coal faces. Most were at least three-quarters of a mile away, and some even required as much as a mile-and-a-half's strenuous walking, carrying all our implements. Conditions underground were extremely primitive, with poor ventilation and inadequate pumping, which resulted in long sections of the tunnels being ankle deep in an oily, black, evil-smelling sludge. This obscured the rails on which the coal trucks ran, which was particularly dangerous in those sections where there were central, continuously running wire hawsers to which trucks were attached. Through lack of proper maintenance and wartime shortages, these were festooned with barbs of broken steel strands that ripped the ankles or calves of anyone unwary or unfortunate enough to place a foot in the wrong place. In addition to that, water was constantly dripping from the roof and sides, and there were secondary falls of rock and dust when pit props shifted.

The reason why the pit props shifted soon became obvious. We discovered that, in their haste to reach the daily quota of coal, some of the Korean and Japanese miners would take props from approaches to the coal face to support the immediate area of their work. It was therefore commonplace to encounter gaps in the lines of pit props (where one instinctively moved faster to avoid a possible fall of rock). Fortunately, our contingent of prisoners included a substantial number of Welsh miners who were able to impart their expertise to the rest of us and avoid a number of potential dangers. Nevertheless, many accidents did occur under the harassing and irresponsible conditions countenanced by the Japanese. By the time we were finally released over twenty men had died, and many others had been severely injured working underground, mostly through the total incompetence of the Japanese overseers. (The only consolation was that some of the overseers also died, just as needlessly.)

Our captors divided the work into ten-hour shifts over stretches of a full ten days before a *yasume*, or rest day. The long walk underground, coupled with another walk of over a mile from camp to pits, plus the shiftwork pattern, inevitably meant that it was an exhausted party that spent the rest day in camp. After the essential chore of cleaning one's clothes it was generally a matter of getting as much sleep as possible before the next shift was due.

At the coal face itself the usual procedure was to drill the rock face with a compressed-air drill ready for blasting. This was a back-breaking job, with blunt drill bits which subjected one to teeth-shattering vibration along with a spray of oil and water from the drill. Each hole drilled had to be at least two feet deep, depending on the type of rock, and usually six or more holes were considered necessary before the Jap engineers tamped in the charges and wired them for blasting. Everyone then retired down a side gallery some distance away while they blew the rock face – which was a very chancy business, since the blasting sticks were always of dubious quality and misfires were frequent. There were some concessions to modern technology in the form of conveyor belts and coal-cutters, but these were constantly breaking down due to poor maintenance and lack of spares.

After blasting, it became a manual, pick-and-shovel opera-tion to clear, first, the vast pile of shattered rock and, secondly, the exposed seam of coal. We were constantly berated by the *hancho*s for failing to remove odd sticks of unexploded blasting powder which found their way onto conveyor belts or trucks, but in spite of their surveillance we tried to ensure that as many of these lethal items joined the outgoing loads of coal as possible, so that they would finish up in the bunkers of ships and railway engines with, we hoped, dire results. It was one of the few ways in which we could get back at the Japs for the primitive and dangerous conditions to which they were subjecting us daily.

In an effort to boost coal production, every shift, whether of Koreans, Japanese or PoWs was given a daily production quota to meet of ten trucks a shift. This was no sinecure, as the trucks in question held ten hundredweight each, and it required super-human efforts from PoWs, many of whom were in truth in no shape to do even half a day's work. Resourceful as ever, the

British overcame this problem by simply 'stealing' trucks from their competitors. It was the practice to assemble all filled trucks at a marshalling point before they were hauled to the surface, and chalk symbols were marked on each truck to show the nationality of the work party. Given any suitable opportunity, a PoW would swiftly rub out the markings on a Jap or Korean truck and substitute our own. Not wishing to push our luck, though, we restricted this to one or two trucks per shift only – we knew the educational standards of the Orientals were pretty low, but we always had to consider that there might be the odd bod who could count up to ten. To further confuse the issue, we often changed Jap symbols to Korean and vice versa. There was no love lost between the two groups, as we quickly discovered, and we often exploited the resulting friction to our fullest advantage. It was a measure of our disruptive skill that they never really cottoned on to what was happening, or, if they did, they were never able to catch our chalkers in the act. There is no doubt that some of the sickest men in our parties owed their lives to this practice, as it released them from having to meet the quota and enabled the 'fitter' amongst us were to cover their inability to work as hard.

Mid-shift meals consisted of a small quantity of cooked rice with the inevitable *daikon* or minute slices of pickled cabbage, conveyed in *bento* boxes or flat tin dixies. These were usually stacked in a recess in the mine workings a little distance from the coal face, to avoid too much dust contamination. The Koreans and Japs had their particular niches where food containers were deposited. On one occasion a hungry PoW raided the Japanese cache while they were at the coal face and ate at least three men's lunches before carefully returning the empty boxes to the pile. When the Japs discovered their loss they immediately suspected the PoWs, and we were all lined up and subjected to a furious interrogation, including an inspection of food tins to see whether any prisoners had any uneaten food. Fortunately, everyone's container, including the culprit's, was as clean as the proverbial whistle.

Everyone was individually threatened and even offered bribes of cigarettes to encourage an informer to split on his comrades, but to no avail. With considerable nerve, the actual culprit then volunteered that he had spotted two Koreans in the vicinity of the Japs' rations. This was more than enough for the Japanese to believe it was true. They regarded ration-stealing almost as a treasonable offence, so, gripping their pick shafts, scurried off to the adjoining gallery where the Koreans were innocently feeding and proceeded to knock seven bells out of them. Naturally, the Koreans did not take this kindly, and the resulting affray lasted for several minutes, before the Japanese emerged victorious. Bearing all the marks of the conflict, they returned to the British prisoners, laughingly boasting that the Koreans now knew who was boss! We nodded sagely.

This was yet another case where, among all nationalities of prisoners of war, the British appeared to have a reputation for honesty and fair play. Although the Japs had a natural suspicion, they would frequently accept our word against others – as in this instance. It is fair to say that, since becoming captives of the Japanese, who seemed to practice all forms of deceit and evasion, we ourselves had abandoned all normally acceptable relations with them. Through sheer necessity we had become part masters of subterfuge and embroiderers of the truth, resorting to stealing anything from our captors or engaging in any other clandestine activity if it meant furthering our own ends or hampering their war effort.

There were, unfortunately, fewer opportunities to practice subversion in camp because there was so little time available between sleeping and working. Nevertheless, we tried to build a working radio. Notwithstanding intermittent searches, materials were smuggled into camp. By this time I had joined a small party working in the heavy electrical department of the mine workshops, where one could gain access to wire and other items essential to radio construction. The guards would run their hands over our bodies and search inside hats and food tins, but on numerous occasions I successfully carried insulating tape, wire and other small components in the clenched palms of my outstretched hands – which, amazingly, they always seem to overlook. Despite our efforts, though, hostilities ended before we could get the radio working.

We had been introduced to a lengthy list of punishments awarded by the Nippon Government for various misdeeds – among them terms of up to ten years' solitary confinement for striking a Japanese soldier, or death by beheading for escaping or being in possession of a radio. Shortly after this notice was served, two British officers in an up-country camp were discovered operating a clandestine set and subjected to hours of horrific torture to try to make them implicate others. This they steadfastly refused to do, although their bodies had been beaten until they were almost unrecognisable. In their rage the Kempetai officers ordered their men to drag the almost lifeless bodies, face down, back and forth over the gravel path in front of the guardroom; this was done by relays of guards for nearly two hours before the Kempetai ordered a halt. Even after this treatment both officers were found to be still alive, but incapable of any reply to the screams of their torturers. Finally the Kempetai, tired of receiving no response, dragged them to the rear of the guardroom where they were flung into the latrine pit and drowned. After incidents like this most prisoners of war would cheerfully have strangled any Japanese military personnel with not the slightest twinge of conscience.

CHAPTER 14
The Shaft

The party working on the 'new' shaft probably had the most thankless task of all the work parties at Kamoo. Those working in the pits had plenty of hazards to contend with, but in the winter they were at least sheltered from the elements, and temperatures below ground were often considerably warmer than those on the surface. The luckless shaft party, though, had to endure cold and wet conditions continuously, whatever the weather. The shaft had originally been started before the war by a Swedish company and then abandoned when war broke out, after reaching a depth of 800 feet. With a surplus of cheap, expendable labour available in the shape of prisoners of war, our captors had restarted the project and intended to reach a seam of essential coal, regardless of cost. The shaft was a large hole about 25 feet in diameter, the sides of which were progressively concreted as it drove its laborious way downwards.

Access for both men and materials was by a giant steel bucket, into which eight to ten men could squeeze and be lowered by cable to the depths below, and two trips provided the tools and materials for the party to spend nearly ten hours hacking with picks and shovels at the mixture of rock and clay that formed the shaft bed. The whole shift was spent ankle deep in cold water, which was continuously replenished by dozens of jets springing from the shaft sides, all the way to the top. A solitary pump barely managed to cope with the flow, and steel hats and oilskins had to be worn at all times. When sufficient spoil had been excavated and hauled to the surface, steel formwork was bolted around the circumference of the shaft, and cement (mixed on the surface) was lowered and poured around it to form a permanent lining. This monotonous and soul-destroying chore continued until our release, by which time the shaft had reached 1,500 feet deep.

As air raids became more frequent, another trial was added to the shaft party's burden. Power cuts occurred, and that frequently meant being stranded below for hours without light or any means of being winched up. Worse, it meant that the water pump was out of action, and once the rising water had reached the chests of the workers before the power was restored. On one occasion the bucket lifting men back to the surface stopped halfway during a power cut, and they were left swinging hundreds of feet above the bottom in pitch darkness, drenched with water falling from the springs in the shaft sides. There were many accidents at the shaft workings, but only one fatality, when an unfortunate prisoner missed his footing in the blackout and fell to his death.

We were lucky to have a Dutch doctor allocated to our camp, but his access to medical supplies was seriously curtailed, and his diagnoses and treatment were frequently overridden by an igno-ramus of a medical corporal provided by the Japanese 'for our welfare'. One of the shaft party reported sick with malaria but was refused exemption from work by this corporal. When the half-delirious PoW arrived at the shaft workings, the civilian overseer regarded him as a potential hazard and sent him back to camp. This infuriated the guard commander, who forced the sick man to kneel on a piece of bamboo pole while holding a heavy rock above his head. After only a few minutes of this torture, the luckless prisoner fainted, only to be roused again with a bucket of water and the process repeated. When the guard commander tired of this, he ordered two of the sentries to beat up the prisoner until they were exhausted.

After this inhuman onslaught the battered remains of the PoW were flung into a cell and left all night at temperatures down to -5°F (-20°C). Despite repeated requests from the British CO and the Dutch doctor, permission to see the prisoner was refused until late the following evening, when examination showed he had several broken ribs as well as numerous cuts and bruises, and pneumonia had set in. Miraculously, he recovered and accompanied me on our eventual return home, but it is little wonder that he had a hatred for the Japs and all they stood for years after the war.

———

During the first winter in Japan, one party was allocated the task of modifying a railway line between these two coal mines. Years of slag tipping had formed an escarpment about forty feet high linking the two pits, and a narrow-gauge railway ran along the top to carry coal, pit props and other materials to and fro. It used small electric locos, but, anticipating future disruption of electric power, and with a supply of coal ready to hand, the Japanese decided to provide a couple of small steam locomotives to do the haulage. It was understood that these were coming from the Philippines, where the gauge of the rails was 4ft 8½in, and we were to lay an extra rail to enable the steam engines to haul the narrow-gauge trucks without the need to modify them to the larger gauge. Every other sleeper had to be removed and replaced with a longer one, using extra ballast manhandled from the nearest slag heap. Rusty, frozen rails, dated 1918 and stamped 'Krupp von Essen', were then laboriously bolted together and spiked to the sleepers.

The distance between the mines was nearly two miles, and the escarpment was open to the freezing winds that blew down the valley. By this time we had been issued with second-hand Japanese jackets and breeches along with threadbare greatcoats, but none of them did much to keep out the bitter winds. Our solution was a lining of cement bags under the jackets, which helped to make up for the deficiencies of our diet and create a semblance of warmth.

Somehow the rail party completed its unpleasant task, and the extra rail remained unused until the following spring, when the steam locos finally arrived. To the chagrin, not to say rage, of our captors, both turned out to be one-metre gauge and unsuitable for the enlarged track. Nothing daunted, the Japanese decided to alter all the valve-gear and axles on the engines – rather than simply relay the entire track – and both were consigned to the main pit workshops for the necessary modifications.

Some of the ex-railwaymen among us could have told them this would be a complex operation, and so it proved. It was many months before the finished engines were rolled out ready to take up their new duties. Several of us were then detailed to clean and polish the locomotives ready for their despatch to the pithead, and by dint mainly of elbow grease, cotton waste and cement powder (in the absence of proper cleaning materials) we produced a result worthy of a *concours d'élégance* at Swindon railway works. Alas, it all came to naught. During a particularly heavy air raid that night, a thousand-pound bomb fell, with pinpoint accuracy, between the gleaming engines and reduced them both to a heap of scrap metal!

Another soul-destroying task during the early days at Kamoo camp was transporting a large Lancashire-built boiler from the main railway depot to the pithead boiler-house, a distance of around two miles. The existing narrow-gauge railway had no trucks anywhere near big enough to move the boiler, which was some 25ft long and 10ft in diameter and weighed several tons, so they decided we would have to manhandle it all the way! The boiler was loaded onto a crude, heavy wooden sled and, with crowbars, rollers and a primitive capstan-type winch, it took a gang of perspiring PoWs two full days of back-breaking toil to drag this mass of steel uphill to its destination. After this and other such tasks we came to sympathise with the slaves of Ancient Egypt.

CHAPTER 15
Spanners in the Works

Opportunities for sabotage abounded, although the penalty for detection was dire, and we were careful not to endanger comrades in the mine, where frequent breakdowns caused delays without any assistance from us. In fact, the general ramshackle quality of equipment and indifferent maintenance allowed us to get away with a number of things that would otherwise have made the Japs suspicious.

The Japanese themselves contributed greatly to the wear and tear of machinery by ruthless usage and lack of essential lubrication and proper adjustment. They were suffering many defeats and subsequent lack of supplies, and general shortages meant that drills, coal-cutters, pumps, fans and conveyors often operated without their full complement of bolts or safety guards and often depended on bent nails and wire. Much damage was also caused by blasting that was so haphazard that it frequently buried essential equipment under tons of rock.

I did not have to spend all my time down the mines, thank Heaven, as a call went out for those who had certain skills to work on the surface in the workshops. I volunteered and thus moved into an electrical workshop, where a party of us were now permanently engaged in coping with the spate of damaged equipment that emerged from the mines for repair. These activities embraced all mechanical equipment from 600hp winding engines to small ventilating fans.

Originally the PoWs' work was limited to cleaning, stripping and preparation before the actual repairs were done by Japanese engineers. However, as the passage of time and the call-up decimated the Japanese workshop staff, the maintenance section was soon almost exclusively manned by PoWs, with only two ex-servicemen in charge who had been electricians of a kind and were discharged from the Nippon Army due to disability. Of course, this afforded many opportunities for discreet sabotage, and most machinery that we 'repaired' seemed to have a very limited working life before it returned to us for further attention. One of our number was well versed in electro-mechanical engineering, so we were able to introduce numerous little defects into mine equipment without detection.

A favourite ploy was to insert old hacksaw blades in the insulation between the coils of winch motors. Bench tests at the works without a load would pass muster, but when the motor was installed at the mine, it only needed the Jap winchman to overload the haulage cable, as he usually did, and the motor would promptly burn out. Also, equipment with gearboxes, such as coal-cutters and haulage drums, came in for periodic overhaul, when the gears were repacked with reconstituted grease into which old nuts or bolts were embedded. Again, during bench tests the grease would remain solid enough to support the foreign bodies within, but in continuous use at the mine it would melt, and the bolts would drop into the cogs with dire results, the resultant mess of smashed and stripped gears and iron filings effectively masking the true cause of the breakdown. These were just two of many acts of indirect sabotage carried out during our time in the mine workshops.

When I first went into the workshop the place was only around a tenth full of the engines, but our sabotage was so successful that by the end of the war you could hardly move in there. And when the machines went back to the mines they were in use for such a short time that shifts had to be curtailed and the men sent back to the surface, so every little helped.

One of the two Japanese in charge of our mechanical tasks was a shell-shock case, invalided out of the Nippon Army, and his disability made him very unpredictable. On the mornings he arrived with a sweat-band on his forehead and a wild, Samurai-like look in his eyes, we expected a bad day. He would throw things at us for no apparent reason or deliver blows for the most trivial offences, and we learned to avoid him like the plague when he was in that kind of erratic and schizophrenic mood.

Frequently he would become morose and non-committal, hiding himself in a remote corner of the works and leaving us to our own devices. He would merely ask us to warn him if the works boss arrived (like most of his countrymen, he was mortally afraid of his superiors). It was during these 'off days', when we had precious little supervision, that we took advantage of any opportunities literally to 'throw a spanner' in the works. At the time we gave little thought to the consequences of our actions and merely accepted it as the least we could do to get back at our taskmasters and, in one way or another, retard their war production.

The other overseer, called Hirano, was a much more amenable and friendly person. For example, if someone in our gang was not feeling that well, Hirano would tell him to go and rest by the warmth of the furnace that was kept going in the workshop, stay there until the end of the shift and be excused from work for the day. Naturally, he would never tell his bosses he had done such kindnesses to prisoners, or he would have been beaten and perhaps even taken off the job. That kindness eventually extended to the very end of the war, when he invited some of us back to his home in the village for a satsuma and green tea with his wife. Some fifty years later, when I returned to Inatsuki with my son John, we were once again invited into his home for a satsuma and green tea and a chance to recall a very different time in both our lives. Of course, we still pulled the wool over Hirano's eyes while we were in the workshop, in spite of his kindness towards us, but that was simply because our allegiance had to be to our fellow prisoners, who were still down the mine and who did not have anywhere near the 'comforts' we were experiencing on the surface.

Occasionally, those of our less fortunate colleagues who were returning from night shifts down the mine were able to contribute to the score against the common enemy. All the loaded trucks of coal filled by previous shifts were hauled along the escarpment to where there were a series of winch-operated drifts or sloping rails to convey them to the main line below. The last day shifts would normally leave ten or more loaded trucks on each slope, held in check only by the winch brake and ready for lowering by gravity in the morning. Usually only two guards accompanied the night shifts of PoWs back to camp, and frequently they would march together at the head of the column, chatting – they probably thought we were all anxious to get back to camp on a cold night, ready for a meal and some rest, and so would not dawdle. This made it possible for the last man – covered, of course, by his companions in front – to gently knock up a restraining brake lever or two as he passed. By the time the loaded trucks had gathered speed down the incline, the work party was well away and in sight of the camp.

The chaos when the mass of trucks and coal reached the bottom of the incline and hit the closed points on the mainline had to be seen to be believed. Coal, twisted rails and shattered trucks spread over hundreds of yards of the mainline railway, and the morning shifts of PoWs had a 'holiday' from going down into the mine while they cleared the debris. To the Japanese this meant delays on the mainline tracks, loss of coal production and another massive repair bill, but rarely were there any repercussions other than their foul temper, as the fault was inevitably blamed on failed brakes and ratchet springs. Had they kept up some semblance of regular maintenance, it would have been far easier to blame what had happened on us prisoners, so we were able to turn their engineering incompetence to our advantage.

Amazingly, Red Cross supplies were finally issued to us for the first time in November 1943 and consisted of a consignment of food and clothing. The food delivery, however, was pitifully small, consisting of one 'individual' parcel (intended for one man) to be divided between no less than thirteen prisoners. During the two years of our captivity in Japan, we each received the equivalent of only six of these parcels, which contained sufficient food for one week for one man. Unfortunately, the value of this precious food was diminished by the Japanese insistence on opening all tins immediately, presumably to prevent us hoarding them against a possible escape. Also, certain items were invariably missing from the parcels, such as chocolate and cigarettes, which the guards openly consumed or smoked. Medical supplies were another essential commodity regularly purloined by the Japanese. (Throughout our sojourn in camp I can remember only one issue: some cough mixture, which apparently the Japs tasted and did not fancy. Whether or not they had a cough, everyone queued at the Dutch doctor's room for a daily spoonful until, after seven days, the supply was exhausted. It tasted like nectar after the monotony of a rice and soup diet.)

Hot water was always available, as the local supply was unfit to drink unless boiled, but some local tea was available in small quantities. This was referred to as 'privet leaves' and was dried after use, being mashed again and again until all semblance of colour was brewed out. (This is probably the reason why I can now drink any tea of whatever shade!) A variety of experiments, intentional or otherwise were tried to augment our food supply. Once an unwary snake was killed near the shaft and brought into camp for cooking. The few invited to partake viewed it with suspicion, being uncertain whether the poison would affect the flesh. I found it tasted like chicken with a slightly fishy flavour.

On another occasion the Jap quartermaster flung several small, skinned carcasses into the cookhouse announcing that the Nippon Government was giving us a 'rabbito presento'. This constituted a real windfall for us, as our meat intake normally averaged about two ounces a month. To ensure that everyone benefited, the carcasses were chopped up really small and tossed into the communal soup *kwali*. I freely admit that we were not in the least perturbed the following morning, when the gleeful Japs informed us that our 'rabbitos' were several local cats rounded up the previous day for a joke. To their chagrin, like Oliver, we just asked for more!

———⊶——⊷———

The same quartermaster had the wind taken out of his sails on another occasion, when he met his match with a bayonet. Every morning we would awake to his banshee screams as he carried out daily loosening up exercises with a rifle and bayonet. A long earthen incline ran from the cookhouse to the guardroom above, and each morning a PoW orderly would deliver two wooden buckets containing the guards' rations. These were naturally considerably better than our own meagre diet, and woe betide the bearer if any was spilled en route. This Jap sergeant would take a fiendish delight in bearing down on the hapless PoW, brandishing his rifle and bayonet and uttering blood-curdling yells in an effort to make him spill some of the pails' contents. Not wishing to be cut off in his prime, the orderly would normally drop the food pails, trying desperately not to spill anything, and step smartly aside, whereupon the Jap would come to a halt, laughing uproariously. He knew that the unfortunate chap would have to return to our cookhouse to replenish the spilt buckets at the expense of our rations or risk a beating at the guardroom for delivering short measure.

One day on the orderly on duty was a British lance corporal who had specialised in unarmed combat. On meeting the charging Jap sergeant, he carefully put down the pails and stood his ground; he knew from experience that, with only two fingers on the side of the oncoming bayonet, he could overbalance his assailant. This he promptly did, and the surprised Jap finished up in a dishevelled heap, lower down the slope. There was a pregnant silence for about a minute, and the PoW wondered whether he had overstepped the mark, but the Jap sergeant, with a furtive glance up towards the guardroom motioned him to keep quiet and to carry on his journey. Later that evening there was a discreet knock on the PoW's hut, and the sergeant was standing outside the door. Everyone tensed themselves for the inevitable, thinking a severe beating was about to ensue, but, amazingly, the prisoner returned a few seconds later with a carton of fifty cigarettes: a King's ransom in camp currency. The Jap sergeant had given it to him on condition that not one word of that morning's incident ever reached the other guards – another instance of the importance of avoiding loss of face.

Our captors' few concessions included permission to observe Christmas Day as a rest period. In spite of the cooks' ingenious efforts to provide something different, though, there was little to enliven our monotonous diet. The Japanese magnanimously provided one small satsuma per man and a few bottles of watered-down sake, but festive spirit was sadly lacking in the sombre surroundings of our mining camp. For propaganda purposes, a photographer recorded the proceedings, the majority of his pictures being enhanced by grouping all the fittest looking men together, surrounded by the maximum quantity of food and bottles. Despite all this carefully staged preparation, the finished prints were amateurish and would not have fooled anyone.

The Shinto religion is predominant in Japan, and there were several shrines on the roadsides between our camp and various work places. At feast times or seasonal harvests, the locals placed offerings of food or fruit to appease the spirits and ensure a period of good luck or a fruitful crop. Frequently, these offerings would be satsumas or other fruit in season, and the Japs obviously regarded it as sacrilege to touch this food. Nevertheless, passing shifts of PoWs contrived to remove these tempting articles undiscovered and immediately consumed their booty without slackening step.

The Shinto religion is animist, believing in spirits and given to much superstition. Talismans of rice straw, rather like corn dollies, would be hung over doorways or mine entrances and at corners to ward off evil spirits. It often gave us secret pleasure to remove these when we were unobserved and watch the Japs halt and change direction or about turn when certain talismans were missing. These pranks were definitely not appreciated by our captors who, at the best of times, possessed a warped sense of humour. In spite of the grim conditions we endured, many humorous situations occurred, although we had to learn to cultivate a poker face and not laugh at the time, only afterwards in the comparative privacy of our huts.

One example of this was when we were on a pit-prop-loading-detail. We were ordered to move a 30-ton rail truck full of these timbers from the railhead to the pit saw mill. Our party numbered twenty in the charge of a pit deputy, but, try as we might, it would not budge an inch. This, we soon discovered, was because one wheel was chained to the rail on account of a faulty handbrake, but we didn't tell the deputy (who had not noticed it) and for some minutes after our discovery continued to puff and blow as though straining mightily in our efforts to get the truck rolling. This, of course, expended very little energy on our part and wasted a fair amount of time. After about five minutes of fruitless pushing, the Jap was so disgusted at his party of British 'weaklings' that he hailed a passing shift of Japanese miners to show us how it should be done.

Without further ado, they all hurled themselves at the rear of the truck (the chained wheel, of course, was in front and out of their sight). We were ordered to stand back and take notice as with loud yells and concerted effort the frenzied Japs thrust themselves again and again at the immobile truck. Rather than lose face in front of the watching PoWs, they almost sweated blood and risked several hernias in frantic efforts to shift this totally immovable object, until the *hancho* spotted the chained wheel. Since it was our Jap deputy who had enlisted their aid, it was he who received the ensuing tirade of oriental oaths. They finally limped off, leaving our crestfallen deputy to detach the chain and sulk for the rest of the morning; for the remainder of this chore we were careful to avoid him as much as possible and survived to have a good laugh later at his expense.

The pit-prop chore was one of the more unpleasant tasks in the mining area. The timber props would arrive at the coal sidings and be unloaded and manhandled to the nearby saw mill. In transit, the heavy props were secured in bundles with sleeper dogs, large wrought-iron staples about 9in wide, driven in by sledge hammers. The bundles had to be prised apart with a crowbar and all staples carefully put aside and counted, presumably in case we retained them as offensive weapons! Occasionally, the staples would snap off, and the spike of metal left embedded in the log was often difficult to see –the metal was invariably rusty, and the bark obscured the point of entry. Whenever any of these dogs snapped off, the broken remainder would be hurriedly hidden, often in the railway line ballast, as dire punishment would follow if such a breakage was noticed by the guard.

The overseer of the saw mill was a particularly unpleasant type – fat and ugly, like a Sumo wrestler – who revelled in making our lives on pit prop detail as miserable as possible. The props varied from 5in to 9in in diameter, were usually about 6ft long and, when wet, weighed almost three-quarters of a hundred-weight apiece. Our tormentor would not allow two men to carry one between them, in spite of the weakened condition of most PoWs. Each man had to shoulder a prop unaided, the rough bark grazing the skin and every man risking a rupture as he staggered from siding to saw mill. All the time, the work party would be harried and harangued with curses and blows by this obnoxious overseer until the last pit prop was stacked inside.

One particularly memorable day, a large pit prop containing a broken steel spike of sleeper dog found its way undetected to the main saw-bench, where the fat Jap was off-loading cut logs. These were to be made into railway sleepers, and the large circular saw was trimming each side to provide flat surfaces. As the overseer stood facing the saw bench to receive the log in question, there was a sudden shriek of tortured metal as the huge saw momentarily jammed on the embedded spike. The wood was catapulted violently forward into the overseer's corpulent stomach, carrying him bodily for several yards before crushing him against the wall of the saw mill. The resultant power surge in the saw blew the main fuse box door off and showered the surrounding shavings with sparks and molten metal. In no time at all, flames leapt up and threatened to sweep through the mill. The PoWs nearest to a fire extinguisher turned the contents onto the blazing mass, but the disappointing spray of rusty liquid that emerged did nothing to diminish the gathering inferno, and all hands were impressed into a belated bucket chain.

After an hour's frantic effort by the assembled PoWs and the Japanese saw-mill workers, the smouldering remains of the machine and its workshop were finally doused. Only then did anyone, Japs included, give the remotest thought to the crumpled form of the overseer who still lay where he had fallen. He was barely alive, having received severe internal injuries, and a party of his fellow workers carried him off to the nearby hospital, where he died later that night. Life at the saw mill, though never very pleasant, was a little more tolerable after his demise.

The Japanese seemed cruelly insensitive to pain and suffering in others, including their own kind. A prime example of this indifference was illustrated when one of the deputies crushed his foot in the railway points at the mine head. His so-called comrades simply burst out laughing, and it was left to some prisoners to release him and convey the fainting man to hospital. And when one of us crushed his thumb in a concrete mixer, we rushed him to the hospital, the mangled digit still attached by a strip of flesh. When the Japanese surgeon arrived he refused to sew it back on or offer any treatment. He simply grasped the damaged thumb and twisted it off causing the unfortunate patient to collapse; his companions were then ordered to carry him back to camp, where our own doctor bandaged his injured hand.

We all dreaded the thought of serious injury, whether from accidents or a severe beating, as the treatment in the only hospital was medieval to say the least. No anaesthetics were wasted on PoWs except local injections for amputations, and these were often so ineffective that operations were still unfinished when the effects wore off. Several appendicitis operations were carried out where the surgeon obviously relied on the patient fainting after he made the first incision. All dentistry was undertaken without injections, and anyone with any infectious disease was simply not admitted to the hospital and had to remain in camp under the jurisdiction of the hard-pressed Dutch doctor.

The Jap medical orderly held a daily sick parade, but this was usually a farce, as his sole aim was to ensure the maximum number of men was available for work. Whatever one's complaint, the universal treatment was a dose of 'Wakamoto' powder; this consisted of rice polishings and at least had some small vitamin content. Ulcers, boils and other skin complaints were treated with hot poultices of Epsom salts, apparently retrieved from captured stockpiles of British Medical Supplies (not recommended for those of a normally quiet disposition!).

Healing of any kind was a long process, due to our lack of proper food, insufficient rest and the legacy of tropical complaints that everyone suffered from. Nevertheless, our optimism was bolstered by fragments of news gleaned from outside sources and the general attitude of the Japanese, whose increasing gloom and deteriorating attitude became more apparent with every reverse that their forces were now suffering in Burma and the Pacific. That optimism was of course tempered by the thought that we were stuck in the very land that was likely to be invaded, and, as we were undoubtedly considered expendable by the Japs, we feared the consequences of that invasion for those in the camp.

Amazingly, there were some Japanese (usually Christians) who, when out of earshot of their fellow workers, would pass on snippets of radio news and occasionally some rare titbits of food. This was obviously done at some risk to themselves, and also considerable food shortages were becoming apparent among civilians.

———

Then came the day we were told that a Red Cross representative would be visiting our camp, the first and only visit during our captivity. This was preceded by a day off shift work when everyone remained in camp to undertake a massive clean-up and receive replacements for ragged clothing. The cookhouse was loaded with extra vegetables and unheard-of joints of meat and baskets of fish.

On the day of his arrival, the Swedish Red Cross officer was accompanied by an entourage of Japanese officers and press photographers who conducted a farcical tour of the newly cleaned camp and its environs while all the inmates remained stiffly on parade. Only our British officer was allowed a few brief words of greeting before the whole procession was whisked away and the camp returned to normal. That same evening the Jap quartermaster removed all the surplus food from the cookhouse, and we were straight back to rice and watery soup. No one had had the opportunity to raise any complaints, although from our emaciated appearance it must have been obvious to the Red Cross representative that all was not well and it was all a bit of a show for his benefit.

A chronic shortage of mail was only one of the pressing matters we would have liked to discuss with him but it was not to be. It was not until mid-1944 that our first delivery of letters was received, and, in my own case, my first from the family, and the forerunner of only twelve to reach me intermittently over the remaining months of captivity. These 'letters' were generally postcards, limited to 25 words only, but they were our first tenuous link with friends and families in the outside world, and treasured as such. A concession gained by the Red Cross visitor was the provision of pre-printed cards for us to send home. These were limited to three or four stereotyped sentences, such as 'I am well, I hope everyone at home is well', etc., the only personal note allowed being one's signature.

We thought these cards might suffer the same fate as had overtaken the previous exercise of this nature, but several of these cards were despatched during the following months, although few ever reached England. We later heard that the very first consignment of prisoner-of-war mail travelled by a long and circuitous route through various neutral countries before finally reaching South America. From there an aircraft took off for Shannon Airport in Ireland but unfortunately crashed on landing, destroying many of the precious written cards. By some miracle, my first letter card was in one of the few oil- and mud-soaked mailbags recovered, and so my family's first communication from me was delivered as a tattered remnant of soggy cardboard on which the address was barely legible. After painstakingly cleaning the reverse side, my father was just able to distinguish a signature which was sufficient to tell them that I was still alive somewhere, although just where, he only found out when I returned from captivity.

CHAPTER 16
Beginning of the End

In June 1945, through various clandestine sources, we learned of the cease-fire in Europe and began to weigh up our chances of release after nearly three-and-a-half years of captivity. It was encouraging to hear of Allied successes in the Pacific and their inevitable progress towards Japan itself. Now that the Germans had been dealt with, we hoped it would not be long before the Japanese received their come-uppance. Nevertheless, many of us were pessimistic, as with every reverse of Japanese fortunes conditions were worsening by the week, and we knew we prisoners were an expendable embarrassment. By now severe shortages of every kind had reduced the local civilians to scarecrows, hardly distinguishable from us. One consignment of Red Cross supplies received at this time contained some Canadian overcoats, gloves and scarves, but we were not allowed to wear them outside camp, even in the bitterest weather, for fear of arousing resentment among the local population, who were clad in rags.

The staple diet of rice was even further reduced, sometimes being mixed with barley, millet or beans to eke out the diminishing supplies. Our daily ration now consisted of a microscopic portion of cooked rice (or substitute), enough to fill a 4oz tobacco tin at each meal. At breakfast, this would include a cup of hot water (tea had disappeared from our 'menu' in early 1945). The midday meal of 4oz of cold rice would normally be eaten at work and would include one thin slice of radish or similar unappetising vegetable. On return to camp the same 4oz measure of cooked rice would await us at the cookhouse, together with a small bowl of hot seaweed soup. All vegetables had now disappeared from our supplies, supplanted by bales of black seaweed. This produced a particularly revolting brew that looked and tasted like iodine, but our doctor pronounced it fit to eat, and we demolished it – there was nothing else. This monotonous diet persisted for the three months before our final release, and we lost weight progressively.

Air raids were now becoming commonplace, disrupting work both above and below ground because of the consequent power cuts. In August 1945 American aircraft showered the whole area of the mines with leaflets warning the population of an impending invasion. These ingeniously used maps of the Pacific arranged like a clock face: each figure on the dial showed a Japanese possession that had fallen to the Allies, the last being Okinawa at 11.55 a.m. Twelve noon was of course Japan itself, and the position of the clock hands ominously implied that the mainland was the next and final target.

Not far from our camp was an airfield from where *Ohka* (*Baka*) flying bombs and *kamikaze* planes operated. Such was the shortage of trained airmen that schoolboys of sixteen were being press-ganged into service as suicide pilots. After a crash course on gliding (no pun intended), the unfortunate youngsters would be strapped into glider bombs secured to the underside of conventional bomber aircraft and flown off to contact the approaching Allied battle fleets. On sighting the enemy, the bomber pilot would release his glider load, and its luckless occupant's one-way mission was to dive his craft into the nearest ship. The inexperience of the teenage pilots and the ungainly weight of the 500lb bomb in the nose led to most Baka gliders coming to a sticky end in the hail of anti-aircraft fire, and they were not so devastatingly successful as the piloted *kamikaze* planes.

All the same, the area's schools were continuously scoured for fresh recruits, and we became used to the daily procession of solemn-faced youths with black kimonos and sweatbands on their foreheads, preceded by a Shinto priest and an air force officer on their final journey to the waiting aircraft. A vast pile of warheads for the glider bombs had been assembled alongside the runways, and the gliders themselves, being made elsewhere, were brought in by rail and assembled on site.

Back at our camp, a deep tunnel had been driven into the adjacent hillside as an air-raid shelter (some parties of prisoners were detailed off to nearby towns to dig further shelters and fill in bomb craters after air raids). In addition to the camp shelter, a slit trench was cut high above the entrance to accommodate the doctor and stretcher-bearers in case a direct hit closed the entrance to the tunnel. As the raids increased, it became a regular occurrence to take shelter in the dark, cavernous tunnel, which contained nothing but a duckboard floor. Everyone in camp, including the bed-ridden, would be herded into its unlit recesses until the 'all clear'.

In spite of the drastic reduction in rations, all men our captors considered fit enough to walk were still expected to continue working ten hours a day in ten-day stints. As one of the 'walking fit', I was detailed as a stretcher-bearer during air raids, and so shared the slit trench instead of going into the gloom of the tunnel below. In practice, we often found ourselves pushed out of the slit trench when things warmed up and spent some interesting hours watching our own aircraft in action while our guards kept their heads down.

On 9 August we set off to work in the usual way, but at midday an area alert caused us to be hurriedly marched back to camp. This was the forty-seventh air raid in the past thirteen days, and so far most Allied activity had been high-altitude bombing. Today, though, we saw smaller aircraft roaring at low level through the mountain valleys, and we dived into our air-raid shelter on entering camp. As usual, the slit trench was full of cowering guards, and the two of us in the first-aid team took our customary positions on the grassy banks above. It was obvious that the war was now reaching a critical phase, for we saw aircraft with the familiar roundels of the RAF racing through the valley. We reasoned that these could only be carrier-based planes from a task-force within striking distance of Japan. 'It can't be long now,' we told each other.

Soon after the Allied planes disappeared we heard and felt a thunderous explosion, which we took to be from the stockpile of bombs at the nearby airfield. Looking down the valley we could see a vast mushroom cloud of smoke slowly rising hundreds of feet into the sky. It was an awe-inspiring sight. Not until two weeks later, when we were released, did we discover that what we had thought was a local explosion was in fact the atom bomb dropped on Nagasaki, over 40 miles away to the south-west (the first had fallen on Hiroshima, some 120 miles north-east of our camp, some days earlier). We also found out later that evening that, since we were in a valley, the blast and heat was partly chan-nelled up the valley and past our camp. When the bomb exploded some of our party had been emerging from the mine covered in coal dust, and the coal dust immediately ignited. Others had the presence of mind to push them into nearby puddles face down, which ensured that they were not seriously injured.

The last cataclysmic air raid lasted until 1 a.m. in the morning, and a cold, hungry crowd of prisoners finally returned to their billets for some much-needed sleep. Mercifully, there was no roll call at the usual time of 5.30 a.m. Instead the Jap Commandant declared a holiday. The next day, too, was one of total inactivity, and – since two consecutive days of rest were unprecedented – rumours began to fly around the camp. Later on the second day the parties who had left camp to dig air-raid shelters elsewhere began to return, bringing the exciting news of a new bomb the Allies were using and of negotiations for peace between Japan and Allied representatives in Tokyo Bay. The guards were now noticeably friendlier towards us, even offering to buy our Red Cross clothing. A few days later, on 17 August, we awoke to an unfamiliar silence from their guardroom and discovered that the garrison had departed overnight – rather hurriedly, leaving all their rifles and equipment. The Japanese Commandant, Lieutenant Takata was found in his office looking rather worried, but on receiving assurances of his personal safety, agreed to accompany our sole British officer to make an announcement on parade. Standing on a wooden box and addressing us in a mixture of pidgin English and Japanese, he announced that the war was now over. In the meantime, he would be grateful if we would assume responsibility for his safety and the running of the camp until Allied troops arrived.

This was undoubtedly the most momentous day in the whole of our captivity. So many times had rumours of peace and freedom been dashed during our long years of imprisonment that we almost could not believe that, at last, this one was true. Curiously, there was no wild cheering, instead many a lump came to the throats of the assembled prisoners and an overwhelming sense of relief like nothing before swept over one's senses. Men were turning to each other silently shaking hands, patting backs, and many had tears streaming down their drawn faces. Hardened though we had become to most of life's extremities at the hands of our utterly appalling Japanese captors, this was one occasion when inner emotions could not be suppressed.

After a night's sleep it was wonderful to awake as free men, and the floodgates of excited chatter opened in joyful expectancy of going home to friends and families once more. Wiser heads prevailed, though, for we were not out of the woods yet. We were surrounded by a potentially hostile community, many of them in as parlous a state as we were for food and clothing. The whole country was in chaos and disruption, due to intensive bombing and the aftermath of Nagasaki and Hiroshima. Our camp food store contained only enough plain rice to last us five days at the Japanese ration scale, and there was no prospect of receiving further supplies. Fortunately, a few Red Cross parcels had been discovered in the guardroom store, and these were carefully divided to provide at least one tin of meat or fish between each pair of men. Guard rotas were formed from the fittest men, to provide some security on the food store and man a main-gate piquet armed with our late captors' discarded rifles.

Next day, a Red Cross official, accompanied by a Japanese interpreter, visited the camp and confirmed details of the surrender, adding that arrangements had been made with the local radio station to establish contact with the nearest allied base on Okinawa Island. It appeared that only the Japanese Military Police were being allowed to bear arms under the direction of the Allies, but, that in all other respects, ex-prisoners of war were to regard themselves as an army of occupation until the Allies could land and take over the necessary administration. We contacted General Macarthur's HQ in Okinawa, stressing the urgency of the situation regarding food, clothing and medical supplies, and were assured that emergency measures were being undertaken to supply us by air drop. In the meantime we were authorised to commandeer any transport or labour we required and to mark out dropping zones in the vicinity of all camps. Air-dropped supplies were to be the only immediate means of relieving our shortages, since all airfields and ports were unusable until clearance squads could land. There followed a delay of three days as we anxiously awaited the arrival of the American relief planes and our food store diminished rapidly, until at the end of the third day only enough remained for one more meal.

Meanwhile, we reflected on past times, when we had subsisted on boiled leaves and grasses and experimented on any kind of wildlife that could be caught and popped into the pot. Those were days when we had never been sure of our next day's meal; now it was different, and no one was complaining at the thought of another hungry period, because we were assured of something soon. The next day we received the welcome radio message that we should expect an air drop at around 2.30 p.m. Every 'fit' man in the camp was mustered at the dropping zone to recover the supplies. (It was indicative of our atrocious treatment by the Japs that, of the 250 inmates of the camp, only 70 were considered anywhere near strong enough to form the recovery party). We ranged ourselves around the perimeter of the marked out area – a parade ground about 200 yards square and about the same distance from our camp boundary.

Promptly at 2.30 p.m., the roar of aero engines heralded the approach of the first of our winged saviours, and then a wave of tremendous excitement ran through us all as we caught sight of its vast silver shape bearing down upon us. The sound of its four huge engines reverberating from the mountainsides, an American B-29 bomber swept over at 500 feet, and every man cheered and waved hysterically as it passed. After this preliminary recce, the bomber receded into the distance, climbing above the surrounding mountains and banking for a second run. This time the massive bomb doors were open, and the pilot flashed his landing lights to indicate that he was about to drop his first load. He had throttled back the engines but was overhead in an instant, and a dark shower of heavy objects descended – as we prudently dived for any cover available. They were oil drums loaded with food and secured to parachutes, but many of the parachutes broke loose from the drums as they fell. For the next few hazardous minutes as free-falling drums crashed around us with sickening crumps, interspersed with overloaded parachutes travelling at double the normal landing speed. We picked ourselves up and looked around, and it soon became clear that the bulk of the drop had overshot the marked drop zone by a considerable distance. We had hardly begun to retrieve some of the undamaged drums before a lookout's shouted warning drew our attention to a second aircraft roaring up the valley towards us. On its first run over, this one dropped a weighted US Air Force shirt with the names of all its Texan crew written across the back and a footnote to say that they would return in a few minutes to deliver a second load. This time, discretion being the better part of valour, we dispersed well away from the DZ but we need not have worried. This load, also dropped from 500 feet, was even more haphazard than the previous one and landed in the area of the nearby Japanese village.

At this point it occurred to us to return to camp to warn the others to take cover, as we did not want anyone, literally, 'killed by kindness'. But we found everyone already safely ensconced in the air-raid shelter, including the patients from our sick bay! Apparently, one free-falling drum had smashed into the hospital, luckily missing those within, and a second had demolished half of the cookhouse roof, crushing a *kwali* full of boiling water in its path. There had been some narrow escapes but no casualties. That was more than could be said for the nearby village: nine of the flimsy wooden houses were completely demolished, with several of the occupants seriously injured in the debris, and a couple had been killed.

The supplies had fallen over a wide area, and we urgently needed to organise collection parties with some local transport so as to salvage what we could before wholesale looting by the locals began. Teams comprising six Japanese and one armed PoW each – plus the only transport to hand, a horse and cart each – were hurriedly sent in all directions to retrieve as much as possible before dusk. Some of the supplies had been damaged by free-fall dropping – the contents literally pulverised beyond recognition – while more had plunged into lakes or had already been broken into by the time recovery parties arrived. For two or three miles around parachutes festooned trees and outcrops of rocks, and even these were being systematically cut down and spirited away to provide clothes for the local population. Nevertheless, enough was recovered from the two drops to provide all the prisoners of war with unheard-of luxuries of food and medical supplies enough to last several days.

Precautionary notices were enclosed with the food advising us to be circumspect over our intake until our systems became used to a normal diet. After all the years of deprivation, introducing our bodies to too rich a diet too quickly could result in a painful death. Happily, common-sense prevailed, and it was a supremely contented band of ex-PoWs that settled down that night after our first decent meal for nearly four years. Another radio message advised us of another air drop in two days time, when more food (and this time clothing and boots) would be part of the cargo.

About this time we thought it would be expedient to have a pictorial record of camp personnel as proof of our prevailing physical condition. Accordingly, a deputation from the camp sought out the local photographer whom our captors had commissioned in the past to record camp events. He was then 'persuaded' to take several photographs of emaciated groups of ex-prisoners; these were subsequently helpful to investigating officers of the War Crimes Commission and provided most of us with grim evidence (if we ever needed reminding) of our parlous condition at the time of our release.

CHAPTER 17
PoWs in Occupation

Before our second air drop we had marked out the dropping zone more clearly and added the legend 'British POW 250' to indicate the number of inmates and help our suppliers assess the amount of food and clothing required. We had already forgiven our American friends for the first, indifferent drop; it had caused much ribald and unrepeatable comment from our RAF PoWs, but we did appreciate that, for pilots used to high-altitude bombing, flying their four engined monsters on supply drops at 500 feet in narrow mountain valleys they had never visited before was no sinecure. (Later we also learned that the hurried assembly of food and other stores had necessitated improvised methods of despatch; there weren't enough cargo chutes, so loaded containers, generally oil drums, were attached to personnel parachutes designed for considerably lighter loads.)

When the second delivery was due, I waited for it sitting on a large concrete roller on the edge of the DZ. The first plane arrived and discharged its shower of parachutes, one of which, as before, broke away on opening. One of the falling drums was heading straight for the concrete roller, and there was no shelter within a hundred yards! In a split second I dived off one side of the roller and hugged the earth. There was an almighty crump, and the roller shuddered as the drum hit the tarmac on the other side and concertinaed. I immediately realised (a) I had chosen the right side of the roller, as I was still alive, and (b) I was deluged in tomato soup, several hundred tins of which had burst on impact. My companions raced up expecting the worst and were not entirely reassured to see my dripping figure. I squelched back to camp for a quick cold shower and then returned to carry on with the retrieval and join in the mirth at my misadventure!

An hour later a second aircraft appeared, supposedly carrying the bulk supplies of expected boots and clothing, closely followed by a third. They roared over our DZ with bomb doors open, and we could see that each bomb bay was crammed with large wooden platforms consisting of heavy timbers bolted together in the form of a raft. These were piled with bales and cartons of supplies and secured to the bomb release gear with improvised webbing straps. The aircraft made their second run, again in line astern and with barely a hundred yards between them.

At 500 feet they released their platforms, which fell free, and for a brief moment the sky was black with falling objects, as bales and cartons broke free of their straps and fell in all directions. And in the centre of the cloud of supplies the supporting rafts, each weighing several hundredweight, descended with a whistling, rushing noise like a large bomb. Everyone scattered as the rafts shattered into matchwood on impact and large bundles of every conceivable size and weight bounced and thudded into the ground over a radius of a quarter of a mile. One unfortunate Dutch PoW from another camp was decapitated by a free-falling carton of, ironically, medical supplies.

After several laborious hours, we finally accumulated most of the undamaged bundles in the camp and took stock of our latest windfall. We found we had enough for six US uniforms apiece, eight pairs of boots and toiletries to last every one of us more than six months! We never discovered whether our American friends were overgenerous, or their quartermasters mistaken in assessing our needs. At all events, we had far too much for our immediate use, so we sought to redistribute it to others who might not have been so lucky.

We knew from the British Red Cross delegate who had visited us earlier that some unregistered punishment camps existed in the hinterland, and we decided to try to contact any in our area. Small parties of PoWs (usually three to six men, preferably with some knowledge of Japanese) set off to seek these camps and arrange for distribution of our surplus to them. I accompanied one party, and, equipping ourselves with ration packs to last a few days, we set off in a commandeered truck full of food, clothing and medical supplies. As a precaution, we each carried identity armbands in Japanese and side-arms (rifles were retained in camp for our own guard duties). There were still some belligerent civilians about, and not all Japanese troops had been disarmed – in fact, in some of the remoter parts of the mainland, the surrender terms were not yet recognised.

Like most civilian trucks, our commandeered vehicle ran on producer gas generated by a Heath Robinson appliance attached to one side of the cab. By feeding this at regular intervals with low-grade coal, we managed twenty miles an hour on the straight, but the truck jibbed at the slightest incline, so everyone had to get out and push. Eventually, after enquiries to local inhabitants, we were directed to a large camp containing about 3,000 Chinese prisoners. There were no guards in evidence as we approached, and our truck drove through the gates to be surrounded by a ragged multitude of scarecrows who cowered away from us as we dismounted. They looked not unlike the pictures one later saw of survivors of the German concentration camps. They eyed us with suspicion and fear, more especially because of our unfamiliar American uniforms, and we had considerable difficulty in making them understand that we were friends. Attempts to converse in English, Malay and Japanese drew no response until one of us tried French, which one of the Chinese who had lived in Indochina could understand. He told us the majority of his fellow prisoners had been captured during the Sino-Japanese War in 1938 and had been subjected to an appalling existence of unbridled cruelty and forced starvation that made our own experience pale into insignificance. Once he explained to his comrades that we were British and had come to tell them that they were free at last, the crowd cheered and virtually overwhelmed us with hugging and back-slapping.

No volunteers were needed to unload the precious supplies, and it was patently obvious that, even fully loaded, what our truck could carry was woefully inadequate to cope with the needs of these 3,000 inhabitants. We promised a return visit the following day, and we also notified the area radio station of the camp's location, so that an air drop could be arranged for them.

I did not accompany the second lorry load of supplies. Instead I went with a party to the port of Moji, where we had originally landed in Japan and where there was another prison camp containing friends separated from us two years earlier. By this time some of the railways were running again, and we hitched a lift to the main-line junction at Fukuoka. Here we found the station besieged by hundreds of civilians and soldiers, all apparently trying to return to their homes after the cessation of hostilities. After about an hour's wait a train steamed into the station, already full to the doors, and as it rolled to a standstill the waiting crowds surged forward, forcing themselves in the carriages until it was almost bursting at the seams. The unlucky ones hung on the footboards along the sides and clambered onto the roofs or anywhere else a foothold could be found. We thought our small party was going to be out of luck until a harassed railway official shepherded us to the engine, where we were installed on the tender and footplate. Thus began a unique journey where the Japanese engine-driver and his assistant invited us to take turns in stoking and driving. During the eighty-mile run to Moji we passed ample evidence of the devastation caused by Allied bombing, and everywhere groups of Japanese were busy clearing debris and erecting temporary shelters. Eventually we arrived at Moji, looking rather like a batch of chimney sweeps, and made our way on foot towards the sea-front prison camp.

As in most Japanese towns, the combination of heavy bombing and incendiary raids had razed most of the flimsy wooden buildings to the ground. But the prison camp, formerly a YMCA building, was a solid stone structure and had survived the worst of the air raids. In its forecourt was a motley collection of vehicles (apparently all the roadworthy ones that were left, including the local fire engine). The resident PoWs had taken General Macarthur's message literally and commandeered everything on wheels that was still capable of moving, along with several drums of aviation spirit. An old saucepan was being used to dispense this highly volatile fuel with into the petrol tanks of the assembled transport, with surprising results, especially on those which had formerly run on producer gas.

Our comrades at Moji camp had also received air drops and were well supplied with all the essentials of life, so we exchanged news and yarned well into the night, and finally enjoyed a night's sleep tucked up in a pile of salvaged parachutes. Our return train journey the following day was not so crowded, and we succeeded in getting a compartment to ourselves. This did not stop several opportunists trying to gain entry at every crowded station en route, but they mostly desisted when given their marching orders, emphasised with the sharp end of a bayonet – the sort of orders we had suffered for too long at the hands of their compatriots.

One thick-skinned individual waylaid us in the corridor for our signatures on an application form which he had drawn up recommending himself as an interpreter when the Allied occupation troops arrived. We all obliged with various *noms de plume*, ranging from Donald Duck to King George the Sixth, and added a footnote that read (I paraphrase): 'To whom it may concern, please kick this character's backside as far as Kingdom come.' We had little doubt that the first American to read it would get the message and, we hoped, act upon it.

———————

Returning to our own camp at Inatsuki, we took our turn at guard duty, which was still necessary to prevent incursions by the locals. We noticed half a dozen heavily armed figures cautiously approaching the main entrance. When challenged they identified themselves as an advance party of paramedics who had been dropped some distance away with the object of contacting us. This was our first sighting of modern GI battle-dress, and, although the wearers were from a medical team, they were armed with automatic rifles and hand grenades. They explained that these precautions were because they were uncertain what kind of reception they would get when they landed.

The team consisted of two Americans, two Australians and two Dutch NCOs, and they soon gave us the up-to-date news, including details of the two atom bombs that had hastened the Japanese surrender. After treating some of the most severe cases in our makeshift hospital, the team recorded details of everyone in camp, including the cases of ill treatment we had suffered during our captivity. After staying overnight, they moved on to contact other camps in the area – after assuring us that every effort would be made to repatriate us, now that our location and numbers were known. We were urged to be patient, however, as communications were still chaotic, and the damage to ports and airfields was seriously impeding the landing of Allied occupation forces.

The civilian population and masses of disbanded troops were desperately short of food, shelter and medical supplies. It was easy to appreciate their misery and feel for them a pity rarely shown to us when in similar circumstances. We heard the local Japanese hospital was crowded with patients, many of them casualties from recent air drops, and, as we had plenty of food and clothing, we thought it would be the Christian thing to do to share it with them, so our commandeered truck was again piled with cartons and set off with an escort of six PoWs. We drew up and unloaded before of the imposing frontage of Fukuoka Hospital. Like most Japanese efforts at ostentation, the pseudo-Grecian facade was just that: it masked a collection of forlorn wooden huts reminiscent of our own prison camp. Conditions inside were absolutely deplorable, with patients herded together on the floor, regardless of sex, infection or injury. The breakdown in supplies meant that the inmates' families were bringing in what little food they could spare, for nothing was being provided by the hospital, and (in a country where people are normally very conscious of their own cleanliness) most of the bed linen, bandages and clothing was unwashed and stinking, and no attempt had been made to clean the floors. The operating theatre was a bare concrete-floored room with a single sink and an ancient operating table, on which a woman was undergoing a Caesarean operation attended by a harassed doctor and two nurses; its swing doors had long ago jammed open, and several young children and a wandering dog passed through the theatre while the operation was in progress. The theatre staff showed no surprise at these visitors, nor at our appearance in the doorway, so we assumed that this was normal. Eventually we found an official who spoke some English and who gratefully accepted our consignment. As a priority, we indicated which was the disinfectant included in the medical packs, for the whole place stank like an abattoir.

(A year later, when I was at Papworth Hospital in Cambridgeshire for rehabilitation treatment, I was looking through the visitor's book and noticed the name of the chief medical officer of Fukuoka, Japan, who had headed a delegation that visited in 1938. Looking at the frontage of Papworth Hall, one can see where he got the inspiration for the facade of Fukuoka Hospital – it is an exact copy!)

About this time, a party left the camp to try and make contact with a satellite camp in Nagasaki, where some of my own unit had been interned. We had heard reports of the drastic effects of atomic bombing, but even our recent paramedic visitors had no first-hand knowledge of the conditions at Hiroshima or Nagasaki, as they had flown in direct from Okinawa. Some of the men originally sent from our camp to dig air-raid shelters had been transferred to Nagasaki harbour to excavate submarine slip-ways out of the headlands; we later found out that other camps, too, had sent men to work in this area. On the morning of the atom bomb raid some 200 PoWs were crossing the bay to the excavations by ferry when the Nagasaki atom bomb burst in mid-air. Sadly, there was not one survivor from this particular craft.

Unaware of this tragedy, our party travelled nearly eighty miles down the valley towards the main harbour but on the approach road to the city we were halted by Japanese military police at a roadblock manned by a detachment of heavy machine-guns. Although, surprisingly, showing no animosity to us as the former enemy, the Japanese commander made it clear that no one was to be allowed in or out of the city, not even ourselves. His orders were to shoot anyone attempting to leave, such was the fear and uncertainty towards the radioactive victims of the holocaust.

A few technicians and doctors in protective clothing had been allowed into the ruins, checking with primitive Geiger counters and trying to alleviate the suffering of the hordes of burn victims. These we could see massing about a quarter mile away, where they had been halted in their frantic attempts to flee the devastated city. Many were dead or dying on the spot for lack of specialist attention for their terrible burns, and only the menace of the machine-guns prevented them from streaming unchecked out of the city.

It was pointless trying to enter the city, so we returned to camp concluding that we could expect no PoWs in that area to have survived. To our surprise and delight, though, we subsequently discovered that a fortunate few had been left behind in the Nagasaki camp to prepare the evening meal for the returning workers; they had taken shelter in a small concrete cellar when the air raid siren went off and had miraculously escaped both the initial blast and the subsequent radiation. All survived to accompany me back to England having suffered no ill effects. I have little doubt that it was the seaweed diet that ensured that they (and we – who undoubtedly experienced the radiation, even 40 miles away) were not affected by the radiation, as the iodine effectively blocked it.*

---

* Now, some 65 years later, I have never having suffered any cancerous side effects. Meg Parkes, whose father you will recall was with me at Tandjong Priok, has been investigating this aspect of our lives in conjunction with the Liverpool School of Tropical Medicine. It is not without significance that, as a precaution against possible radiation attacks, British troops serving in Afghanistan have been issued with seaweed pills.

CHAPTER 18
Starting Homewards

Three weeks had passed since the surrender, and still we had seen no Allied troops except the paramedics who had visited us earlier. But some progress had been made, with a limited landing of US construction engineers at Nagasaki where clearance was in hand to prepare the way for disembarking reinforcements. We were now ordered to make our way there, where arrangements would be made to take us off by ship to bases where proper rehabilitation and medical treatment was available. A few days then elapsed while rolling stock and a steam engine were found to transport our entire contingent, including all our sick, to the embarkation point.

By now everyone was naturally getting more and more impatient to shake the dust of Japan off our feet and get started on the road home. Curiously enough, in spite of the treatment we had undergone (particularly from some of the more sadistic mine deputies), we bore little animosity towards our ex-masters. Rather, we felt sorry for the terrible predicament they were now in.*

---

* Not all PoWs felt the same, though. Some Americans who had been singled out by the Japanese for consistent ill-treatment were not so forgiving and decided to leave their mark before leaving Japan. A party

Those of us who had been in the mine workshops decided it would be a nice gesture if we off-loaded some of our surplus food and other goodies to the Japanese with whom we had worked, for there had been a few (though not many) who had treated us with a measure of respect. As we entered the workshops carrying a sizeable pack of supplies we discovered, sitting in a corner, the old enemy who had made our lives a misery with his psychotic moods. Seeing us, he made as if to run off, but we were in the way, so he cowered down, expecting, no doubt, to get the full treatment from his former whipping boys. We presented him with one of our parcels and told him it was a parting 'presento', and we did not intend to beat the living daylights out of him. At this he broke down and cried, and we left him a ragged pathetic figure, mumbling thanks as the doors of that place of so many unpleasant memories closed behind us for the last time. Goodness knows what became of him.

The next day we learned that a train had been assembled and would call for us in the morning, so, settling down for our last day in camp, we prepared for an early move. At 2.30 p.m. our reverie was shattered by the sound of approaching aircraft, and we rushed out to see three large bombers overhead. Someone had clearly boobed back at US headquarters, for the turning aircraft proceeded to offload the heaviest consignment of materials yet on our dropping zone! This time the drop was much more accurate,

of them accordingly visited the next village up the valley from our camp, where several mine deputies were known to be housed. Fortunately for the Japs, word of the avengers' approach preceded them, and they found only an empty village. Nonetheless, they systematically wrecked or set fire to all the houses before they left.

but it took the concerted efforts of the entire camp to recover all packages and move them to safety.

By the time we had finally assembled the plethora of provisions into huge stacks on the parade ground it was nearly dark, and a check revealed that sufficient stores for 2,500 men had been dropped. It was then obvious that this was intended for the large Chinese camp some distance away, and that the pilots had used the wrong grid reference. Since we were leaving early next morning, we sent the Chinese a message with details of the drop and advised them to send a detachment to guard the stores before the whole site was looted.

With few regrets, we paraded next day in our new US uniforms, carrying rations for only one day. Picking up those on stretchers, we slowly marched off towards the hated camp gates for the last time. But one lad cried 'Stop!' and ran back into the Mess hut, to reappear seconds later holding up a gramophone record for all to see.

'This is it,' he cried and dashed the record to pieces on the ground before the approving company. Then, having symbolically burnt our boats, we passed out of the gates.

The story behind that incident had started several weeks earlier when a local Jap businessman, no doubt hedging his bets on the future, presented the camp with an old gramophone and six records. Five were in Japanese and almost incomprehensible to our ears, but the sixth was in German and featured 'Turkish Patrol' on one side and 'The Song of the Flea' on the other. For lack of any other entertainment, these two tunes were played interminably during the following weeks until everyone was heartily sick of them. In spite of this, the record bore a charmed life and survived to meet its inevitable doom only as we left.

Our long column moved out and down the dirt road to the railway depot, and we could make out furtive shapes assembling on the surrounding hillside. These were undoubtedly members of the local population preparing to descend upon our camp like a horde of vultures. After about a mile of slow progress, determined by the pace of our stretcher-bearers, we met the advance party of several hundred Chinese hurrying towards our late 'home'. We stopped to update them on the situation and advised them to occupy the camp as quickly as possible, but they needed little urging. Most were armed with pick handles and short lengths of piping, and they broke into a trot with howls of glee at the expectation of a clash with their former captors. There was precious little love lost between the Chinese and the Japanese at the best of times, and we shuddered to think of the mayhem that would result once the two sides met, though we could make an educated guess which would come off worst.

We had a last look back at the gloomy pithead workings at Inatsuki as we entrained at Kamoo station. At the final count, there were about 200 ex-prisoners in our rail party, and we carried with us 22 urns of ashes, a grim reminder of the unfortunate chaps who did not make it – some, sadly, had actually died since the surrender.*

---

* We later handed these precious urns over to the War Graves Commission for burial. There had been no cemetery at our camp as, in accordance with Japanese custom, all bodies were cremated. This had been carried out in a furnace resembling an old-fashioned baking oven just outside the camp perimeter, and it was considered an honour by

After some three hours of stop/start progress, our train finally approached the outskirts of Nagasaki, which by now had been reported safe for access. Only now were we able to see at first hand the terrible devastation caused by an atomic explosion. Most of us were no strangers to large-scale bombing, having seen the havoc wreaked by the Germans in the Blitz, but what confronted us at Nagasaki was awesomely and uncannily different. The mid-air burst had created an effect that I could only compare to a giant scythe. Almost everything seemed to have been cut off about three feet from the ground, and anything still standing above that had been scorched as if by a giant blow-torch. Reinforced-concrete buildings and chimneys had retained their steelwork in the form of crumpled bird-cages with odd fragments of cement still adhering. On the adjacent railway tracks and city tramlines, the detached bogies of rolling stock still remained, as did the cleared station platforms, but the entire trains of engines and rolling stock, together with trams and other road transport, had been swept up into a mountainous tangle of twisted steel against the hillside.

Acres of open space strewn with piles of rubble and smouldering debris showed where the residential areas had once been. Apart from the odd civilian picking his way among the rubble, there was little sign of life, and everywhere there was an eerie silence. Most of the dead we saw were unrecognisable, lying where they had been at the instant of the explosion.

the Japanese for the deceased's best friend to apply the match to the piled wood logs under the corpse.

In the harbour sunken ships and floating debris were spread across the entire water surface, and it was hard to see how any craft could find its way through. We detrained on the dockside, where US engineers had bulldozed some clear spaces and erected prefabricated huts with 'US Medical Corps' stencilled on the sides. We had our first foretaste of American efficiency when we were briskly ushered into these to be showered and dusted with DDT before receiving a complete new kit of clothes. Any personal effects we wished to retain were quickly and efficiently decontaminated in a mobile disinfector, but everything we had worn previously (even the relatively new air-dropped uniforms) was promptly burnt.

An American doctor graded us into two parties, with the most serious and stretcher cases being loaded onto a small tender that had come alongside. Standing well out to sea, we could see the outlines of a large American hospital ship towards which the tender swiftly made its way. The rest of us, about 150, were detailed to board a large destroyer that had slowly nosed up to the dockside as we completed our decontamination procedures. Before boarding we were treated to the rare luxury of coffee and doughnuts dispensed by a smiling American nurse, the first white woman many of us had seen in over four years. We were so tongue-tied at this radiant apparition that the doughnuts and coffee were consumed almost mechanically as we gazed in wonderment: how different from our reaction to the Japanese nurses at the time of our enforced injections!

The destroyer, of a type none of us had ever seen before, was the USS *Cofer*, a 'close-support destroyer' designed specifically for landing marines near inshore targets. She carried six large landing craft in davits, and below decks there was accommodation for up to 200 marines in triple bunks. Her normal crew numbered 125, many of whom lined the rails to help us aboard. The captain told us over the Tannoy that a hot meal awaited us below, and the ship would cast off once we were all aboard. A narrow channel had been cleared through the floating debris in the harbour, and the *Cofer* steamed very gingerly astern, following as closely as possible the route of her inward journey, and it took some twenty minutes before we reached the open sea. The precaution was necessary because many mines, released from the sea bed by the atomic blast, had floated to the surface and become entangled in the harbour wreckage; consequently, there was no room to turn ships. It became very apparent that we had been lucky when a waiting landing craft entered the harbour via the path *Cofer* had recently used: it was within a hundred yards of the dockside when a thunderous explosion blew its bows and landing ramp right off. Fortunately, the crew were all in the stern quarters and were quickly rescued by a tender.

Once at sea, we set course for Okinawa, about two days steaming from Japan. The hot meal on that first evening afloat turned out to be an early Christmas dinner. The crew had generously donated the store of turkeys and plum pudding that had been shipped aboard for their own celebration because they did not expect to return to the USA until well into the New Year. (This was typical of the many generous gestures we experienced from our American hosts during our homeward journey.) After the meal, a film show was organised for us, the first we had seen since our capture in 1942. A screen had been erected on the fantail stern, and the projectionist operated his machine from one of the rear gun sponsons. The film turned out to be the classic western *Stagecoach*. Halfway through, a tropical downpour drenched everyone on the open deck, including the projectionist – but he soldiered on under the protection of a groundsheet, as it was quite obvious his audience, wet through or not, was not going to leave until the final credits came up!

The next day the crew took us on guided tour of their ship, and we were greatly impressing with the complex array of weapons and all the unfamiliar devices designed for the comfort of the crew. There was a more relaxed attitude between officers and men than would have been seen in the British Navy, and the Captain even welcomed us up on the bridge to demonstrate all the controls and the submarine detection equipment. The steersman was ordered to make a tight turn to demonstrate the ship's manoeuvrability at speed, and as it heeled over sharply a loud chorus of yells and curses came up from the decks below.

'Shucks,' muttered the Captain. 'I clean forgot that it was chow time below!'

On the second day we sighted Okinawa and nosed into a bay full of British and American naval craft, many of which had been destined for the final assault on Japan that, fortunately for us, had not occurred. We were intrigued to see the huge factory ships and floating workshops, which we were told had accompanied many of the land invasions in the Pacific. These massive vessels were capable of processing practically any type of tank or truck and all manner of armaments, from hand pistols to the largest howitzers, no matter how badly damaged: the equipment would be ferried out from the fighting beachheads and shunted into one end of the floating works to emerge within hours at the other end operational and ready for war again.

We passed through this armada and entered a quiet bay where there was no other shipping but a tented camp on the shore. The *Cofer* edged in as close as she dared, and then one of her landing craft ferried us to the tents. A solitary US Marine sergeant met us and invited us to make ourselves as comfortable as possible anywhere we chose in the camp. He didn't know how long we might be under canvas but said trucks would collect us when our journey home resumed.

In the commodious tents we found rows of camp beds, and on each one a carton of 'K' rations sufficient for a week's stay, along with several cans of beer. We soon made ourselves quite at home, and eventually settled down for the night content in the thought that Japan was now far behind, and we were indeed homeward bound.

In the morning, there was little to do except laze around in the sun, sand and sea, for we were left entirely alone. However, we had been warned not to stray too far inland from the camp, as there was sub-tropical jungle above the sandy beaches. And, from the Marine sergeant's account, there were still some isolated pockets of active resistance in the hinterland of Okinawa because some soldiers were still unaware of Japan's capitulation.

About mid-afternoon our attention was caught by an approaching landing craft carrying a large container. When it grounded, the crew of six burly Marines, all heavily armed, dropped the ramp and ran up the beach with a petrol-driven portable winch. They hauled the container ashore under the eyes of a crowd of curious ex-PoWs, mystified as to what military exercise was being put on for their benefit. Having secured the container near our tents, five of the marines re-embarked and chugged off, leaving one to guard this 'secret weapon'. As we watched, he divested himself of hand-grenades, rifle and all his other warlike equipment, including helmet and shirt. Standing in his singlet and slacks, he reached inside a panel on the container's side, produced a white cap and apron, and then dropped the whole side of the box – to disclose a mobile ice cream and Coca-Cola parlour!

'OK, guys! Come and get it!'

We needed no second invitation to sample the creature comforts the average GI apparently expected to have available even close to the battle front. Chatting with the cheery dispenser of this good fare, we soon learned that most amphibious operations in the Pacific had certain priorities. These seemed to be, first, the construction battalions and, second, the cinema and PX canteens – often established within range of the Japanese defenders. Those GIs really knew what close support meant!

That night the camp was inundated by a tropical storm, and we were grateful for the raised camp beds which let the torrential rain flow freely through the tents beneath us. The downpour slackened around midnight, when we were roused by the sound of a helicopter landing on the beach alongside. The pilot brought news that trucks would arrive at dawn to take us to the nearest airfield to fly out. No one slept much for the rest of the night; most of us were too busy packing.

Promptly at first light a convoy of trucks appeared. So did another heavy rainstorm, but we all managed to scramble under the canvas hoods before its full force hit us. I was in the last truck, which took some time to start (the downpour had affected the electrics), and it was not until some fifteen minutes after the main convoy had left that we were able to set off in pursuit.

CHAPTER 19
Flight to the Philippines

After about an hour picking our way over flooded dirt roads, we arrived at a deserted airstrip – it was immediately apparent that our driver had brought us to the wrong destination. There were only two major airfields on Okinawa, so, realising that our waiting aircraft must be at the other one, we set off again and eventually reached it about two hours later.

It was now daylight, and there seemed to be a great deal of activity at the far end of the field where a pall of smoke was rising. We were told two aircraft had come to grief on take-off, each with its complement of returning prisoners of war. The first, a Boeing Superfortress, had burst a tyre just before lift off and cartwheeled, killing all the passengers, the only survivors being six of the crew; this was the wreckage we could see burning. Then the following plane, a Dakota with thirty ex-PoWs aboard, had taken off successfully, but an engine had cut out as it was crossing the nearby coast, and the aircraft crashed into the sea with no survivors.

Our remaining group of ex-prisoners stood silently on the airfield perimeter, each of us wrestling with very mixed feelings. It seemed bitterly ironical that our comrades had come this far, surviving all the vicissitudes and deprivations of prison life, only to be killed on the journey home. And, but for the delay caused by driving to the wrong airstrip, we might well have been on the same aircraft and suffered the same fate. Once more fate had taken a turn that favoured me.

The US Air Force officer in charge of despatching was very sympathetic and explained that we now had the alternative of travelling by sea if we wished, although delays in shipping would mean waiting at least another seven days. Most of our truck's passengers opted to wait for a sea voyage to become available, but six of us decided that, by the law of averages, we should take our chance on the next plane. After all, with our luck, a ship might well hit a mine – there were still plenty of them bobbing about unsecured at that time!

Any reservations we might have had were swiftly banished by the sight of a Dakota taxiing towards us – though we were not altogether reassured by its battered and weather-beaten appearance or the insignia emblazoned on its nose: an angel in flight! We clambered aboard *Angel Ann*, as she was called, closely followed by a group of Dutch PoWs who had just arrived from another part of the island. The crew consisted of one nonchalant, gum-chewing US pilot, who welcomed us cheerfully aboard. The legend stencilled inside the aircraft's door stated that its maximum capacity was 29 passengers, but a quick check showed there were 32 of us, excluding the pilot. This did not concern him unduly, though, and we taxied towards the main runway for take-off. Halfway there, we were flagged down by a pursuing jeep festooned with eight US Air Force personnel. After a brief consultation with the pilot these supernumeraries hauled themselves aboard and announced they were hitching a lift to Manila, our ultimate landing point.

No one spoke, but a few silent prayers were offered as we roared off, both engines on full throttle to clear the smoking wreckage of the earlier crash. At 8,000 feet, the plane levelled off and the pilot laconically told us we could smoke (although since before take-off several of his more timid passengers had already been smoking furiously to calm their nerves). This was my first-ever flight, but any qualms were quickly dispelled by the fascination of studying the sea and the islands below and the novelty of being in an American aircraft. The Dakota was a robust transport used as a general workhorse by most of the Allies, and this example had obviously been doing her stuff all over the Pacific. The interior was spartan in the extreme, with rudimentary seats made of webbing along the sides only. These were sufficient only for the authorised load, so at least ten of our passengers simply sat on the floor without the luxury of seat or safety belt. And the toilet facilities were certainly primitive: a funnel was attached to a short length of hose disappearing into the atmosphere through a hole in the fuselage near the tail! For more pressing needs an upturned GI helmet nestled in an ammunition box full of straw at the rear of the plane's main compartment. It needed some acrobatic skill to use either of these appliances, especially in the bumpy air over the mountains of Luzon in the Philippines, where sudden drops of many feet could occur without warning.

Our route to Manila covered 1,500 miles, and at about the halfway mark, someone noticed a considerable oil leak from the starboard engine. This was brought to the pilot's notice, but he seemed only mildly irritated.

'Hell, not that again,' he said, 'I thought they'd fixed it for good last time.' Then, after a short and pregnant silence, 'Keep your eye on it, fellas, and let me know if it starts smoking!'

We never found out what he would have done if it had, for, happily, Manila airport appeared on the horizon within half an hour. That engine was now sounding decidedly rough, and we had a very bumpy landing in consequence. I thanked the pilot for bringing us safely down and asked what would have happened if that engine had failed in mid-air.

'Well,' he said, 'I guess we coulda ditched alright, as this old crate would float for about six hours. But I woulda felt kinda mean about you guys, because I have to confess ma dinghy only holds one!'

From Manila airport we were bussed to a large tented camp on the outskirts of the city which had been specially set up to receive returning PoWs from all over the Pacific. Teams of Allied doctors and nurses were on hand to check all incoming drafts and give treatment where necessary. No effort was spared to provide complete rehabilitation facilities and prepare for the final despatch home of the many nationalities of ex-prisoners likely to pass through their hands.

To bring us up to date with our four-year backlog of news and events, a large information centre had been set up containing both current and back numbers of magazines and newspapers, and documentary films were available at the camp cinema. The information centre was staffed with Red Cross representatives to answer our many and varied questions, not least requests for news of our homes and families. An accumulation of mail awaited us, and each ex-PoW was allowed a cablegram, so that the glad tidings of his arrival at Manila could be rapidly wired to nearest and dearest.

Apparently, our party was one of the first to fly in from Japan. Again we had cause to thank our lucky stars, when the news of yet another air mishap was broadcast. The next plane to leave Okinawa after ours had been a Boeing Superfortress carrying thirty Dutch ex-prisoners. There were no seats in this bomber type, so most of the passengers were seated on the fuselage floor and in the bomb bay. During the flight, at a height of 10,000 feet, someone accidentally actuated the bomb bay release, and eight men fell to their deaths into the Pacific below.

After we had been allocated a tent of our own, I and a companion made tracks for the central information tent. Coming towards us on the approach road was a woman in uniform accompanied by a British Staff Officer. As we saluted she stopped and introduced herself as Lady Mountbatten, explaining that she had flown in that day from Singapore to help in repatriating prisoners of war.

'Is there anything I can do for you?' she asked 'Or anything you want right now?'

For a moment we were both absolutely tongue-tied and at a loss to reply. Confronted by the wife of the Supreme Commander of the Pacific Area, the first Englishwoman we had seen for four years, a mixture of awe and embarrassment struck us dumb. Her friendly manner soon put us at our ease, though, and in no time we were chatting away like old friends.

'Is there anything I can do for you?' she asked again.

Knowing about all the possible transport delays I asked whether she thought we would be home in time for Christmas.

She assured us that she would do everything in her power to ensure that all British PoWs would indeed be home for Christmas 1945, and her words came true.[*]

The Red Cross, which Lady Mountbatten represented, were energetically despatching as many PoWs home as practicable, once they had been assessed fit to travel. However, this was not easy, as PoWs had a low priority for transport. Large concentrations of troops, predominantly American, had been built up all over the Pacific islands in readiness for the final assault on Japan that never took place. Public opinion back in USA was clamouring for the early return of their menfolk, but this was difficult because of the shipping situation. The vast armada of warships and support vessels were crammed with war supplies and munitions which had to be offloaded before shore-based troops could be embarked; in many cases this meant ships had to return to the States to unload and then return empty to pick up the waiting troops.

The entire logistics of the Pacific war area had to be put in reverse to run down the massive state of preparedness and then return the concentrations of men and materials to their places of origin. Small wonder delays occurred. The inmates of the PoW rehabilitation centre had perforce to leave in batches as and when

---

[*]Some years later I and my wife Lilian were privileged to meet Lady Mountbatten at the annual Papworth Everard flower show. In spite of the ten years since we had first met, and the many hundreds of returning prisoners she must have come into contact with in her work in the Far East, when I was introduced to her (and before I could even mention our previous meeting) she asked: 'Weren't you the man in Manila who asked me whether he would be home for Christmas?' I was speechless for the second time! I can only put this down to the fact that my colleague and I had been the first, somewhat emaciated Jap PoWs that she had set eyes on and it had clearly made a lasting impression on her.

transport became available. This could be either a plane or a boat, and one took a chance on where the journey would end. Planes and ships were leaving Manila daily for India, Australia, South Africa, Canada and the USA, and the object was to get as many of us as possible started on our homeward journey, with a stopover at any of these destinations.

We had been among the first to arrive in Manila, but it was two weeks before we could join a ship to leave it. The time passed quite pleasantly, though, and we did little but relax in the sun and sample the various pastimes and entertainment available in the camp.

CHAPTER 20
Pacific Passage

A party of 200 British PoWs, including survivors of the ill-fated *Prince of Wales* sunk at Singapore, boarded transport to the docks. A brand new US troopship awaited us, its rails already lined with hundreds of returning American GIs: the *Marine Shark* on her maiden voyage from the States. We were the last aboard, and it seemed the crew was in a hurry to depart, because we cast off when the last man stepped off the gangplank. We were told the outward voyage had been a record crossing of the Pacific in thirteen-and-a half days, and Captain was trying to lower this to thirteen days on the way back. Our destination was San Diego, California, and he hoped to make it in time for Navy Day on 27 October.

This being the US Navy, the *Marine Shark* was a 'dry' ship, no alcoholic liquor being allowed aboard. Unknown to the Captain, though, the engine room staff had smuggled a quantity of illicit booze aboard and secreted it around their workstations. As a result, supervision below decks slowly but surely lapsed as their intake of alcohol increased. Some of my fellow PoWs were ex-Navy men, and they were the first to notice that something was wrong with the note of the engine. They went to the Captain to report their concern, but their warning came too late to prevent an engine bearing burning out after twenty-four hours steaming: the direct result of a drunken engine-room rating failing to check the cooling water.

One engine had to be shut down immediately. We were passing Guam, but there were now no facilities there for major repairs to shipping, so we changed course for Hawaii and Pearl Harbor. Running on one engine reduced our speed considerably, so the Captain's record attempt was abandoned, and in altering course we had run into heavy weather. It was now the typhoon season, and our route to Hawaii meant skirting a gathering storm. For the next two days we laboured on at half speed, with life lines rigged on deck for safety, and it became hazardous to cross the open decks. ('*Déjà vu*', one might say!) The cooks were unable to discharge garbage overboard, and soon an accumulation of rubbish cans appeared roped to the stern rails until better conditions permitted their disposal. As the storm worsened and waves broke over the decks with greater frequency a jetsam of food scraps and empty cartons began to wash everywhere, even down the companionway to the decks below. Conditions became even more unpleasant when a diesel tank ruptured on the lifeboat deck, and its contents joined the evil-smelling rubbish swilling around.

As a result, conditions below decks were almost indescribable – not improved by the fact that most of the GIs and even the ship's crew (!) were seasick. Surprisingly, only our contingent of British were immune, and we tried to clear up some of the mess and also do some cooking, since we seemed to be the only ones on board with an appetite! Finally, the ship limped into Pearl Harbor, where a task force of engineers descended into the bowels to start repairs. While we were in dock a clean-up took place – largely carried out by members of the engine room staff, supervised by naval police as punishment for their misdemeanours. Dock staff worked around the clock on the necessary engine replacements, and forty-eight hours later we were on our way again.

The ship's paintwork had suffered during the storm and the drastic cleaning operations, and the Captain decided to paint the ship while on the move. This entailed 'careening' ship: a practice often used by the Americans, which involved moving water ballast to produce a list to port or starboard as required. This enabled the painting squad to use extended jets to spray areas of the hull below the normal water line. With characteristic American speed, the painting was completed in two days – which was just as well, as it was rather uncomfortable moving around or eating meals with the decks tilted at such an alarming angle. At the end of the repainting session, a radio message was received instructing all ships returning to the States to jettison all surplus ammunition and stores. A crisis was developing at ports on the western seaboard: so many cargoes were being returned to the homeland that storage was at a premium, and the accumulated stores could not be transported inland fast enough. For the next twenty-four hours, we ex-PoWs watched with mixed feelings as tons of food, clothing and ammunition were thrown overboard by fatigue parties of GIs.

In the early hours of the following morning, we were suddenly awakened by a grinding noise from the engine room, which was below the British quarters. A petty officer survivor from the *Prince of Wales* went below to investigate and returned to report that, not only were the engine room staff all drunk again but, once more, a bearing had burnt out! This was the last straw for the Royal Navy contingent, and they returned in a body to the engine room to shut down the damaged unit. Meanwhile, the Captain was again notified, and the Master-at-Arms with an escort promptly locked the befuddled engine room staff in the brig. It transpired that these wily chaps had secreted even more liquor in remote parts of the holds than was originally thought.

Locking up his engine-room staff left the Captain with a problem: there was no one left in a fit state to operate the engines. At this point some of our Royal Navy personnel volunteered to work the ship until further notice, and this unorthodox solution was gratefully accepted. After this we had no further problems, apart from returning to half speed on the remaining engine. Ironically, the ship's quartermaster had based his assessment of our food requirements – and therefore what had just been thrown overboard – on the cruising speed with both engines. Now we had jettisoned so much, it was plain that we didn't have enough supplies left to make San Diego. We therefore altered course to make for San Francisco, the nearest point on the Western seaboard, but it still meant the imposition of the very food rationing from which we all thought we had just escaped.

Until further notice our daily food issue was reduced to one tin of Spam between two men, a packet of dry biscuits apiece and coffee. After this announcement the ship's Tannoy system played 'I'm Dreaming of a White Christmas', which didn't go down very well with the assembled PoWs – who by now were definitely feeling fed up and far from home. It was therefore with considerable relief that we saw the morning sun glinting on the Golden

Gate bridge as we entered San Francisco harbour some days later. As we slowed down for tugs to nose us into the approaching docks, one long-serving GI could wait no longer and, to the cheers of his compatriots, dived overboard to swim the last hundred yards or so; as we tied up alongside, his bedraggled figure was seen kissing the dockside tarmac. He did seem glad to be home!

Our party disembarked before the bulk of the Americans aboard. By now we had accumulated a full kit of US Army clothing and quantities of souvenirs and, together with this baggage, we transferred to a large ferry and chugged across San Francisco Bay. We passed the stark outline of Alcatraz Prison on its forbidding rock and continued to the next island, which housed Fort McDowell, a military establishment. Here we stayed for two days, indulging in a surfeit of typical American Army fare and being waited on by Italian PoWs.

After that we took the ferry back to San Francisco and boarded a train for a journey inland. There followed a fascinating journey along the famous Cascade Route through the Rocky Mountains, traversing several hundred miles of the most picturesque mountain scenery on the western seaboard of America via some amazing feats of railway construction. Late that night, we steamed into Tacoma in Washington State, where we detrained into an army camp. The US transport officer there told us our stay would depend on the availability of cross-continental rolling stock, which would convey us to New York and a homeward-bound British ship.

Meanwhile, the hospitality of the US Army and the local town folk was ours, and we soon settled into our new quarters.

Our stay lengthened to two weeks, as the hoped-for trains did not appear due to heavy US commitments and the fact that, understandably, we were a lower priority. Eventually, the Canadian government agreed to take over our welfare and responsibility for continuing the homeward journey, provided we could be conveyed to the Canadian border. This entailed at least another day's journey through US territory to reach Vancouver, and normal railway trains were just not available. The transport officer therefore resorted to a clever ruse. He had a hospital train shunted into the camp under cover of darkness; all British PoWs were then issued with US Medical Corps pyjamas and asked to occupy its bunks as the train quietly chuffed out in the small hours, en route for the Canadian border. Apparently, only hospital trains had priority over other rail traffic!

Only one stop was expected, and we were urged to remain in our bunks in case someone in authority noticed that we were not *bona fide* American hospital cases. To our embarrassment, though, we were met at Mount Vernon in Oregon by a reception party of women's organisations thronging the platform and expecting it to be full of their compatriots. When the train rolled to a stop, hordes of these benefactors boarded the train visiting all the 'bed-ridden' cases and dispensing all manner of cigarettes, fruit and other creature comforts. When they discovered from our accents that we were actually returning British PoWs their enthusiasm knew no bounds, and it required all our self-control to remain doggo in the bunks and keep up the pretence of being immobile because of our 'injuries'!

Luckily for all concerned, the train had only stopped to take on fuel and water, and this somewhat disconcerting episode was over in half an hour. It was quite dark when the train rolled into Vancouver station, and it was a relief to change back into our uniforms and return to normality. But, had it not been for the ingenuity of the chap in Tacoma, we might have been marooned there for many weeks.

CHAPTER 21
Canada, Queen Mary and Home

We did not stay long in Vancouver. A train was already waiting on an adjoining track, with steam up, and we only had to cross the platform. Already aboard was a contingent of returning PoWs who had been landed on Victoria Island by HMS *Glory*, and they told us the train was bound across Canada to meet the *Queen Elizabeth*, which would be waiting for us at Nova Scotia. Also aboard, in the guard's van (or 'caboose'), was an army quartermaster who lost no time in fitting us out with battledress and heavy greatcoats (we were still wearing US tropical kit).

Even in Canada there were travel priorities, and our route was not the most direct one possible but followed the less-used northerly track, crossing the snow line into sub-zero temperatures. The carriages were double-glazed and well heated, but we were warned to wrap up against frostbite whenever alighting at any of the innumerable stops. The cuisine in the restaurant car was equal to any first-class hotel's, and the sleeping/tourist coaches were very comfortable.

This remarkable journey took us, first, through the Canadian Rockies and then circuitously through the vast backwoods and open prairies, giving us all sorts of opportunities to marvel at the fantastic scenery and the engineering feats that made the railway possible. It was scheduled to take five days, and we were making good time until the third day, when a steam coupling burst on the rear coach late at night. As this was on the heating circuit, the half-frozen occupants of that coach crowded forward into the next one and spent the rest of the night bedded down in the aisle. The train then diverted to Winnipeg, where repairs took a whole day before the journey could be resumed.

But when the citizens of Winnipeg realised there was a train-load of British PoWs stuck at the station, their reaction was spontaneous and genuinely hospitable. Many small groups of PoWs were whisked off in cars to spend the day with their hosts, while those left on the train were the recipients of every kind of generosity, ranging from cigarettes and sweets to creature comforts like gloves and scarves.

The following day we steamed away from a crowded send-off, but later heard that, due to the delay, we could not now meet the *Queen Elizabeth*'s sailing date, and our train would be diverted to another port. So we ended up rolling into Toronto, one of Canada's most southerly cities. Here a civic reception awaited us at the main railway station: civic dignitaries and representatives of welfare organisations wined and dined us on the open plat-form until quite late, and we were a merry crowd when we finally returned to our waiting sleeper coaches. While the festivities were in progress our Canadian engine had slipped its couplings, and an American loco took its place.

In the early hours of the following morning we were on the move again, this time back into US territory. At breakfast we passed Niagara Falls and the city of Buffalo, where we entered New York State and followed the Hudson River to New Jersey.

Here we finally detrained and spent the night in a US Marine barracks with the lights of Manhattan Island twinkling at us across New York harbour. After a mountainous breakfast our much-travelled party boarded the ferry *Stony Point* for a trip across the bay, enthralled by the wide panorama of skyscrapers as we approached. The ferry passed the Statue of Liberty and berthed at the Cunard dock where we saw the grand old *Queen Mary*. Her massive bulk towered above us as we transferred from ferry to dockside. Alongside her in the next mooring, though, was the huge American battle cruiser *Missouri*. The Americans affectionately called her 'Mighty Mo', and well she deserved the title, being by far the largest warship we had ever seen – longer and wider than the *Queen Mary*, her masts and radar arrays towering way above the *QM*'s funnels.

It was quite an experience for most of us to board such a famous liner, and in spite of many alterations during her conversion to a troop carrier, she was still a most impressive sight. The vast dining hall was now a mess for 1,500 men, with meals served on a rota. The passenger list was only 3,500, of which 500 were returning PoWs; the rest were VIPs and British service personnel who had been on attachment to US forces. However, the crew told us that at peak periods of the war the *Queen Mary* had carried as many as 22,000 troops at a time across the Atlantic in a five-day dash. Due to her speed, these trips were usually unescorted, and the passengers were delivered without mishap.

The thousands of GIs had inevitably left their mark, though, and considerable wear and tear was apparent everywhere.

Chewing gum by the hundredweight was impressed into the decks and rubber floors of the saloons and cabins; graffiti was everywhere, and the entire teak handrail – over three-quarters of a mile around the ship – was deeply inscribed with signatures. Kilroy had indeed been aboard the *Queen Mary*!

Late that night she steamed majestically past the lights of Manhattan, down Long Island Sound, and we had a last view of the illuminated Statue of Liberty as we set course across the wide Atlantic for the last stage of our long journey home. The crossing was to take five days, and the Captain broadcast a special message of welcome to all returning PoWs, giving his permission for us to move anywhere in his ship. This did not go down very well with the VIPs, as most of their lounges and sun decks were marked 'Out of Bounds to Troops', but naturally this did not deter us from making a tour of inspection.

Most PoWs had by now accumulated two kit bags, one Canadian and one US, which had been carefully packed with many essential goodies for our folks back home. These items included nylons and other rationed goods we had been told were scarce in Britain. So my partner and I were very concerned that we had lost sight of our kit bags during the loading procedure. We had seen them come aboard in a loading sling, so we reasoned that they must have been hidden away by someone with an ulterior motive. The freedom of movement the Captain had given us was therefore a boon, and we spent the major part of four days visiting every nook and cranny of the ship, including the kitchens and engine room, to try and find our missing kit bags. Not only was this an education in itself, but we were immensely relieved eventually to discover the lost articles under some life rafts on the sun deck. Clearly they had been purloined by a crew member, but we decided not to leave them where they were and wait and see who it had been when we got back to England – we took them back to our cabin under lock and key.

At the end of the crossing a thick fog denied us the beauty of the approach up the Solent to Southampton. Even though it was 5.30 a.m., the rails were crowded with expectant PoWs, eager for their first glimpse of any light that would indicate the shores of home. Most of us had been away for four long years, and in some cases (where regulars had been on station in the Far East) it was five or six years since they last had last seen the shores of Blighty.

Muffled up and cold as we were, it was a very emotional time, and most of us were wrapped up in our own silent thoughts, remembering those comrades who had not had the luck to make it and lay buried in some far-off jungle cemetery or were returning in small caskets of ashes. My companion was a hard-bitten Birkenhead lad, a blacksmith in civvy street. One of the toughest characters in my unit, he had suffered greatly at the hands of the Japanese, but had never been known to crack or show any emotion. As I glanced at him tears were streaming down his rugged face, he turned to me and said, half-crying, half-laughing:

'I never thought I'd be glad to see a real pea-souper of a fog again!'

He shook hands with me silently and turned away.

By mid-morning, the fog had lifted slightly and we docked safely. A line of army trucks took us from the ship to Southampton Common, where there was an army camp, and that evening we were treated to another Christmas meal, even though it wouldn't be December for another couple of days. It wasn't such a luxurious repast as we had had on the *Cofer*, but this was austerity Britain, and we were just thankful to be back home and in one piece.

Travel warrants and clothing coupons were issued, and we all said our good-byes to comrades of the past four years and went our separate ways. At long last, my war was over.

After I had finally collected my demob suit and officially left His Majesty's Service, the tally of active service recorded in my pay book was 'six years and three hundred and thirteen days' (I had originally signed on for six months' militia training and three-and-a-half years in the reserve).

POSTSCRIPT

When I came home I weighed not much more than seven-and-a-half stone (47.5kg), and my time in captivity had affected my body far more than I could ever have imagined. I only realised this when, after six months' recuperation at home, I went back for an army medical, and the doctor said, 'Good God, man! I thought you would be dead by now!' Not what I wanted to hear!

I was lucky that this doctor knew of the work being carried out on TB patients at Papworth Hospital in Cambridgeshire, and so I was sent there, really as a last resort. It was run by the outstanding Dr Pendrill Varrier-Jones, who provided a regime of sunshine, fresh air, light work, surgery and eventually drugs to alleviate the symptoms. Most of these benefits came from being allocated to individual wooden huts, built in the village workshops, which rotated towards the sun. In winter they could be perishing!

The army doctor had originally told me that, if I didn't drink, smoke, lift anything heavy, do any digging, etc., I might even last a year – but I've lasted over sixty more than that! In the bitterly cold 1947 winter, when most of the village's water pipes froze, knowledge and skills from my former profession as a plumber were badly needed, and despite doctors' warnings I was soon working many hours digging up pipes and solving the myriad problems of getting people reconnected. It was during my time at Papworth that I met Lilian, a nurse from the Little Bromwich area, who was visiting her uncle and aunt, and in 1948 we were married at St Peter's church in the village. By now I had a permanent post in the Papworth Industries (where all the fit patients were given work, in what was one of the first sheltered workshop schemes), where I stayed until moving to my present home in Trowbridge in 1960.

When I went back before the army medical board in the early 1950s they carried out all the tests they had done previously and, with some surprise, pronounced me A2 – exactly the same as my rating when I first joined the army in 1941. As a result, the army immediately withdrew my disability pension! Although somewhat taken aback by the verdict, I was simply glad to be alive and grateful for Varrier-Jones's pioneering work, for Papworth and for Lilian for jointly nursing me back to full health. When we moved to Trowbridge we both became heavily involved in the life of Trinity Church, and my faith has played a major part in my forgiveness of the Japanese for what they did to me.

The trip back to my former prison camp in 1995, as part of the celebrations of the fiftieth anniversary of VJ Day, brought back many memories of my time there, and meeting Hirano again was a pleasure (we still correspond to this day, both of us in our early 90s). But the sixtieth anniversary celebrations in 2005 were something to remember for the rest of my life. The honour of being able to present orchids to Prince Charles and the Duchess of Cornwall to be laid on the footplate of the steam engine *Singa-*

pore at the Living Museum exhibition in St James Park was an experience I will savour. Appearing live on BBC *News 24* alongside another PoW who could never forgive the Japanese was topped on VJ Day itself when I was called into the BBC's *Mailbox* studios in Birmingham and, to my surprise, hooked up again on live television with the Japanese Ambassador to the UK. In front of millions of viewers he personally apologised to me for what his fellow countrymen had done. That, I realised, was humbling for him, and also for me. A proper apology to all those who had suffered had been sixty years in coming, and the vast majority of those who should have heard it years ago had already died, but it was made with a sincerity that showed that this apology was genuine, unlike the weasel words and promises we had heard from the Ambassador's compatriots some 63 years before.

A few days later, on Sunday 24 July 2005, my son John and I (representing COFEPOW and FEPOW respectively) were involved in laying a wreath of orchids at the Cenotaph, appearing on global television and national radio for a second time, and then met Prince Charles again in the Palace of Westminster at the reception afterwards – this was the culmination of a very special year for me and my family.

In 2009, a 90th birthday card from Hirano came to the attention of the media and once again I was a bit of a celebrity nationally, even appearing on ITV's *News At Ten* as part of their regular final item of unusual news.

In 2010, a further television documentary team from Japan's NHK television company came to interview me for a programme on survival at the hands of the Japanese military, so life in my nineties still has its moments.

What, though, has been particularly gratifying via my membership of COFEPOW and the JAVA 42 Club (the latter more intimately associated with all those who were captured on that island, as the name suggests) has been the opportunity to give some succour to the surviving relatives of those who fathers and grandfathers suffered as I did for those long three-and-a-half years. Many PoWs would not talk to their wives, or their children or grandchildren, about how captivity affected them. As I have had first-hand experience of what they went through, I hope this has been a cathartic experience for the relatives with whom I have been in contact.

Of course, as time goes on, the PoW camp survivors get fewer and fewer and the FEPOW's remembrance prayer becomes ever more poignant:

'And we who are left grow old with the years
Remembering the heartache, the pain and the tears.
Hoping and praying that never again
Man will sink to such sorrow and shame.
The price that was paid, we will always remember
Every day, every month, not just in November.
We Shall Remember Them.'

APPENDIX 1

*Translation of speech by the new Commandant of
Tandjong Priok Camp in 1942*

I am Lt Siozawa, who has come here as Camp Commandant.

Needless to say, you are all prisoners of war and I am the person responsible for all matters pertaining to you.

All commands given in fulfilling my task have to be strictly carried out. On the other hand, great responsibility rests upon myself in view of the consequences. That is to say, I have to arrange so that you will all return to your native lands and families in as good spirits as before the war.

All my commands will be those natural to the fulfilment of my duty.

I think, as everybody here is, and has been, in the services, you will all understand the demands Camp life makes upon you. Most of you seem to understand this and your behaviour generally is good, but some cannot be said to be good; on the contrary they are far from good. These latter seem to be very casual, especially in their attitude when saluting, which is bad. From the manner of saluting it can be observed whether such a salute is sincere or not.

I have up to now visited many others but never have I seen a Camp where the saluting is so obviously lacking in sincerity – I am very sorry that is so. From this moment on I want you to amend your behaviour and always be keyed up to your best. I especially request you to pay the strictest attention to this point.

I consider adverse circumstances can bring out the better instincts in the men. In this respect this is now an excellent opportunity to improve your ideals.

When I can see that everybody has attained this attitude, I promise to grant you every possible concession in my power. In this connection I am already formulating plans.

In brief I will ask that all orders given upon my authority should be promptly carried out without question and failure to do so will not be overlooked under any circumstances; on the other hand I will not neglect to show kindness to those who merit it.

Finally I think the best thing for you is to bear in mind that you are members of a great nation but also to fully understand your present position and to obey all orders of the Dai Nippon Gun and to await the coming day of peace.

APPENDIX 2

Transcript of document issued at Tandjong Priok
in 1942 for prisoners to write to loved ones

Prisoner of War 9999 (Gunner)

Mrs A.B. Smith
20, Beach Road,
Blackpool, (Lancs)
England

9th November 1942

Dear . . . . . .

I never imagined I should be writing to you from a prison camp.

We all underestimated the ability and offensive power of the Nipponese.

So here I am, with many of my friends, a prisoner of war in Java. The Nipponese are carrying out their international obligations towards us.

I can only hope that the war will soon be over and I long to get back home to you.

(Remainder of letter)

YOU MAY:

1. Say you are in Java.

2. Ask whether your family is getting enough money.

3. Refer to your health or the death of friends.

4. Mention people in the camp

YOU MAY NOT:

1. Mention that we receive pay.

2. Mention anybody who has left the camp or the prospects of further parties leaving.

3. Make any mention of the progress of the war.

(End your letter thus:)

From John Smith
(Name in full)
(NO RANK OR NUMBER)

APPENDIX 3

Names and places of origin at time of capture of
Services personnel in the PoW camp at Tandjong Priok

RANK	NAME	TRADE	PLACE OF ORIGIN
Captain	L.P. Dowdall	Civil Engineer	Soebang, Java
Lieutenant-Commander	H.C. Upton	Admin.	c/o Malayan Establishment Office, Singapore
Sergeant	H.J. Murrowood	Admin.	Wynnum, Queensland
Sergeant	E. Laing	Hygiene	Lavender Bay, NSW, Australia
Sergeant	R.C. Windurst	Fitter	Cardiff, South Wales
Cpl	L. E. Buck	Carpenter	Lamport, Northampton
Chaplain	T.W. Bindeman		South Perth, Western Australia
Bombardier	E. L. Clash	Carpenter	Caerphilly, Glamorgan, Wales

RANK	NAME	TRADE	PLACE OF ORIGIN
Signalman	E. Kewley	Carpenter	Auburn, NSW, Australia
Gunner	E. Steemson	Carpenter	Mansfield Woodhouse, Nottinghamshire
Private	P. Thomas	Carpenter	Bulemba, Queensland, Australia
Private	W.C. Kennedy	Fitter	Mackay, Queensland, Australia
Gunner	J.H. Thompson	Storeman	Glasgow, Scotland
Private	C. J. Morgan	Labourer	New Norfolk, Tasmania, Australia
Gunner	A.P. Bowden	Striker	Melbourne, Australia
Corporal	R. McLaughlan	Blacksmith	Higher Tranmere, Birkenhead
Craftsman	J. F. Baxter	Plumber	Hanwell, London
Gunner	J.C. Howard	Pavior	Saxmundham, Suffolk

RANK	NAME	TRADE	PLACE OF ORIGIN
Gunner	J R. Skinner	Pavior	Egham, Surrey
Lance-Bombardier	J. Smith	Carpenter	Abertridwr, Wales
Private	R. E. Shegog	Labourer	Launceston, Cornwall
Sergeant	L. J. Shorter	Fitter	West Hove, Brighton
Private	C. H. Gale	Carpenter	Finsbury Park, London
Trooper	G. Alton	Plasterer	Chesterfield, Derby
Sapper	R. Armstrong	Carpenter	Somerton, South Australia
Corporal	R. F. Bristow	Carpenter	Queensland, Australia
Bombardier	A. C. Martin	Carpenter	Manea, Cambridgeshire

RANK	NAME	TRADE	PLACE OF ORIGIN
Private	L. J. Bailley	Carpenter	Bellerive, Tasmania, Australia
Driver	W. J. Parsons	Bricklayer	Combe Martin, N. Devon
Private	R. J. Wise	Labourer	St Helens, Tasmania, Australia
Bombardier	R. W. Nimmo	Chargehand	Petersham, Sydney, Australia
		(Labour)	NSW, Australia
Lieutenant	H. K. Allen		Ironbridge, Shropshire
Lieutenant	L. Hunt		c/o Hong Kong Shanghai Bank, Singapore
Sergeant	H. W. Scowan		Clacton on Sea, Essex
Sergeant	D Pymont		Campden, Gloucester
Captain	H.N. Kettlewell		East Harptree, Bristol

RANK	NAME	TRADE	PLACE OF ORIGIN
Sergeant	W. T. Annett		Bruton, Somerset
Lance-Corporal	D. C. Davies	Draughtsman	Harmer Hill, Shrewsbury
Lance-Corporal	R. W. McIntyre	Tinsmith	Queensland, Australia
Private	T. G. Cullen		Hobart, Tasmania, Australia
?	M. H. Croft		Streatham, London
?	A.S.G. Bennett		Catford, London
?	R.B.H. Baker		Wallington, Surrey

(**Author's note:** This list refers to the maintenance department at the largest transit camp in Java in 1942–3. The unusually high number of personnel designated as 'Carpenter' was a cover for certain technicians, notably armourers and radio mechanics, who were engaged in the various clandestine activities referred to in this book. The principal reason for this subterfuge was that we soon discovered that the first Commandant at the camp had been in charge of a Royal Engineers' unit in the First World War. However that RE remit was nowhere near as extensive as the range of activities with which we were involved in the British or Australian services. We therefore decided to trade on his gullibility in believing that our expertise was limited to the given professions.)

APPENDIX 4

Medical report on 8 Camp by PoW Medical 1.9.45

(applies to whole camp)

Medical Officers:

Capt. James A. Gryder Jnr, US Public Health Services,
Washington DC
Lieut. Bareld Jan van de Meer, Officier van
Gazondheid, DVC, Bandoeng, Java.

(1) **PERIOD 13.10.43 to 4.12.43.**

During this period, 251 British personnel were in camp.
PoW medical staff: 1 Sergeant and 1 Private, Royal Army
Medical Corps (RAMC). A Japanese Sergeant was in
charge of medical services and a Japanese Army MO
visited the camp once a week. The British brought to this
camp a fair stock of drugs and dressings including
Emetine, vitamin injections and other valuable drugs. All
this was confiscated by the Japanese, in theory for use in
the MI room. In practice, little of it was re-issued and
then only such things as iodine, quinine, etc. When the
Japanese MO was changed after two months, it was
found that he had taken all the most valuable supplies
with him. The treatment over this period was rudimentary in the extreme and was almost entirely confined to
aspirins and iodine. At this time, the general health was

fairly good (by PoW standards), which was lucky, as apparently the only English that the Japanese MO knew was: 'Never mind, work tomorrow'.

(2) **PERIOD** 5.12.43 to 1.4.44.

On 5.12.43, 151 personnel arrived, including the Dutch Medical Officer, Lieut. Bareld Jan van de Meer. For this period, only a few rags were available for dressings, and, for other treatment, some boric ointment, ichthyol, iodine, diarrhoea powders, aspirin and magnesium sulphate (Epsom salts). Very little was provided for anaesthesia (incisions of abscesses, etc.) and no microscope or laboratory facilities whatsoever. A Japanese Army MO visited the camp once a week. Early in 1944, after three deaths from bacillary dysentery, and many cases of pneumonia, the camp was also regularly visited by civilian doctors from the local hospital (the Mitsui concern) who left prescriptions for the patients.

The camp hospital consisted of a wooden hut – the normal Japanese design, of 8 rooms, with paper windows (*Shozi*), which was very draughty. Patients lay on the matted floor (*Tatami*) alongside each other. There was no warming of the hospital. Two British medical orderlies had to do all the nursing, even with thirty very sick men in hospital, until 23.4.44, when an American MO, Capt. James Gryder, and one American Nursing Orderly arrived in camp.

(3) **PERIOD** 1.4.44 onwards.

On this date, all the Japanese military personnel left the camp, except for the Commandant and one warrant officer, being replaced by civilians, who also took over the medical side. The civilian medical staff consisted of two orderlies whose medical knowledge, by RASC or similar standards, was elementary, and the camp was regularly visited every second day by one or two civilian doctors. Supplies of dressings and ointments now improved a little, and patients received medicine and powders from the civilian hospital. Occasionally, a sample of sputum or urine, and sometimes a blood slide, went to the civilian hospital, but far too infrequently. In cases of accidents, an X-ray was usually taken, and the PoW doctors were allowed a hasty glance at it, but never more than one picture from one position was taken. On July 1944 a new hospital block within the camp was opened, consisting of three wings. Each wing was 75 ft x 15 ft and was divided into three rooms. The building was of wood with glass windows and equipped with wooden beds with a straw *Tatami* on top, so that care for the individual patient was facilitated. There were no facilities for heating the wards, however. Two PoW medical orderlies worked as nursing orderlies, now assisted by one additional man for ward cleaning and other odd jobs; one orderly was therefore released for full-time duty in the MI room. The number of patients varied from twenty to thirty-five.

GENERAL OBSERVATIONS

1. EXCUSED DUTY

Sick parade was a continuous battle between the PoW doctors and the Japanese orderlies to try and get sick men 'Excused Duty'(ED). Every day, a large number of men were sent to work who, by normal standards, would have been ED or even hospitalised. The Japanese orderlies' lack of medical knowledge, and their anxiety to send as many men as possible to work, contributed equally to this state of affairs. A man with a temperature of over 37.5°C (99.5°F) was always ED. Patients suffering from diarrhoea, extremely prevalent in this camp, worked until they were on the point of collapse. Not until three men died of cachexia in December 1944 was any real notice taken of persons in a generally run-down condition.

2. LIGHT DUTY

(a) Until March 1944 the utmost that a sick man could hope for was hospitalisation, or a few days ED, and then he would be sent back to normal work. From this time onwards, however 'Camp Work' was started, i.e. light work in camp, such as gardening and other general fatigues. This enabled a number of old, weak and sick men to have work more suitable for their condition. Although the Japanese orderlies were loath to put men on camp work, the numbers thus employed gradually increased and, for the last months of captivity, included about 15% of the camp.

(b) 'Light Duty Tickets' were issued to workers from March 1944 onwards, but were of little value as the Japanese foremen at work took little notice of them.

3. DYSENTERY

A number of cases of suspected dysentery occurred but, in spite of repeated applications, in only one case was a stool test made – when an officer contracted this disease.

4. MEDICAL SUPPLIES

(a) The drugs supplied by the Japanese were frequently insufficient in quantity. The PoW doctors considered the sulphur dosage for pneumonia patients entirely inadequate (3 grams per day). The range of drugs supplied was limited.

(b) Emetine (or any other treatment for dysentery) was never received, except in the Red Cross medical supplies, of which the following were received in this camp:

December 1943   3 Wooden Crates Cough Mixture

April 1944   1 Crate American Red Cross Type IIA
(deficient of 3 bottles Emetine hydrochloride)
1 Crate American Red Cross Type III

February 1945   1 Crate American Red Cross Type IIA.
(deficient of 3 bottles Nicotinic Acid)

> 1 Crate American Red Cross Type IIB
>
> 3 Crates American Red Cross Type III.

(c) The issue of Red Cross drugs was controlled by the Japanese orderlies, who often refused to issue drugs which the PoW doctors considered necessary.

5. PREVALENT DISEASES

Infections of wounds, boils, phlegmons, diarrhoea and colds comprised 90% of the sick parade. Next came complaints due to malnutrition and vitamin deficiency – beriberi, oedema and cachexia.

6. FRACTURES

Plaster dressing of fractures was very seldom used, and no mechanical equipment for obtaining traction was provided.

7. TUBERCULOSIS

Of nine suspected TB patients, only one was acknowledged by the Japanese to have had a positive sputum test (and this was subsequently said to have been a mistake). In addition, three cases of pleural effusion developed and are regarded as tubercular in origin – though not by the Japanese, although the men concerned were hospitalised. Sputum tests for these three men were refused.

8. OUTSIDE HOSPITAL FACILITIES

Some treatment was given to patients at the local civilian hospital when camp facilities were inadequate. Ten hernia operations were carried out, also some optical treatment, following which spectacles were supplied where necessary. In cases of accidents at work, injured persons were given first-aid treatment here before being brought back to camp.

9. DENTAL

Persons requiring urgent extractions were treated at the civilian hospital but, otherwise, no facilities were available. The camp was supplied with no dental equipment and no PoW dental officer, although both were repeatedly asked for.

10. VACCINATION

All personnel were vaccinated twice in the twenty-two months.

11. INOCULATIONS

All personnel were inoculated against typhus, etc., at about three-monthly intervals.

12. FOOD

Over time, the quality and quantity of food provided gradually deteriorated, but the same amount of work was required from the men. The main features were lack of animal protein and fresh fruit (Vitamin A, B & C deficiency). The Japanese tried to solve this problem with supplies of ox-blood, bones and intestines, in insufficient quantities however, and at extremely irregular intervals.

For some periods, the supply of fresh vegetables was adequate, but, for the greater part of the time, it was insufficient and the quality was poor. A kind of specialist in bio-chemistry supervised the cookhouse for 2/3 weeks in the spring of 1945 and, a short time after, another Japanese doctor carried out a large number of metabolism estimations. No apparent results followed these activities. Probably the most illuminating comment on the whole food question is the fact that, from December 1943 to August 1945, the average weight of the British fell steadily from 60.00 kg to 51.30 kg [see Appendix 5]. In spite of repeated requests, no special food was ever provided for hospital patients – in fact we were frequently ordered to reduce their rations. (Note, in Japan an individual who is unable to work is regarded as a drag on the community and receives scant consideration in the matter of food). However, by setting aside some foods from the scanty Red Cross supplies and by drawing on the camp rations we were able to improve patients' diets a little.

13. SOAP

The supply of soap was inadequate in view of the fact that coal-mining was the main work of the camp. (During the period of one year commencing August 1944, in all, 15 normal-size tablets were issued per man, and this had to cover shaving and laundry, as well as personal ablutions). This resulted in a large number of men suffering from boils and infections.

14. BATHING FACILITIES

These were probably the best feature of this camp. A large communal hot bath was provided with two cold showers. This bath, undoubtedly, saved many lives.

APPENDIX 5

Average weights of British personnel,
No. 8. PoW Camp, Fukuoka

(Before December 1943 no records were available)

Dec. 43	60 kg
21.1.44	58.70 kg
21.2.44	56.90 kg
18.3.44	58.00 kg
21.4.44	57.20 kg
11.5.44	56.20 kg
14.6.44	56.06 kg
12.7.44	56.29 kg
12.8.44	56.28 kg
12.9.44	56.00 kg
11.10.44	55.30 kg
11.11.44	55.12 kg
16.12.44	54.91 kg
11.1.45	55.35 kg
16.2.45	55.93 kg
16.3.45	55.45 kg
20.4.45	53.44 kg
17.5.45	52.94 kg
16.6.45	53.55 kg
15.7.45	52.90 kg
12.8.45	51.30 kg

APPENDIX 6

Report on working conditions – 8 Camp, Fukuoka, Japan, 1.9.45
By Capt. Peter Williams, RA Commanding

The following report is in respect of British personnel. The general remarks apply to the whole camp, however.

1. WORKING PLACES (ALL MITSUI)

(*a*) *Kosaku* – General factory with a large building yard. An average of 20 men were employed in the saw-yard buildings and on general work.

(*b*) *Sanko Denki* – The local electrical shops. An average of 20 men were employed, chiefly in repair and maintenance of electrical machinery.

(*c*) *Tateko* – A deep shaft sunk to meet a drift in one of the local coal mines. 120 men were employed in November 1943, gradually dropping to 40 men in May 1945 when work at this project stopped. Men on top made cuttings, drains, etc., and worked in the forge. Others worked in the shaft itself, where conditions were extremely bad, owing to constant cascades of water from the sides, which resisted all efforts to dam them. The men were provided with capes, but these were of poor quality and failed to keep them dry. Early in November 1943 a large fall took place; miraculously, no one was killed, but the work appeared to be too dangerous (at any rate to inexpert eyes,) for PoWs. Representations were met with the assurance that there was no further danger and that any work engaged in by Japanese personnel was suitable for prisoners. Although no further large falls took place, pieces of rock fell regularly, large enough to have killed anyone directly underneath. One man was killed here when he fell off a travelling platform in the shaft. I attribute this accident to inadequate lighting. A hot bath was provided for workers at the shaft head.

(d) Kofune and Kamoko coal mines – Local coal mines employing the remaining British personnel. Conditions varied considerably from face to face. The men did all types of work – timbering, coal-hewing, blasting, truck pushing, etc. Often the men had to work in water, or in seams 2ft high. One man was killed and one had his spine fractured in II Kofune.

GENERAL REMARKS

1. HOURS OF WORK

(a) Factory, Sanko Denki and Tateko above-ground parties worked on day work, others on shift work, either A.M., P.M. or nights:

SHIFT:	A.M.	P.M.	NIGHT	DAY
Parade for Work	04.45	12.45	20.45	06.45
Work commences	06.00	14.00	22.00	08.00
Work finished	14.00	22.00	06.00	16.00
Return to Camp	15.15	23.15	07.15	17.15

(b) The time allowed for eating food varied according to the Japanese foreman. The average would be about 40 minutes (official minimum 30 mins). No other rest period was allowed (officially) during working hours. Sometimes the period was as little as 15 mins, in which case, representations to the Commandant usually brought about some improvement.

(c) For the first 5 months, there was one day of rest every eight days, but on that day work in camp had to be done, as there were no camp staff to do fatigues during the working period. Men would often return after 8 hours in the mine and would then have to carry coal for an hour. For subsequent periods, rest days were usually 3 a month (although on four occasions only 2 a month) but were less disturbed, as general fatigues were being done by men on camp work. The British worked a highly successful system of unofficial rest days by which, owing to a flaw in the Japanese records, approximately 10% of a shift took a daily rest. This was not discovered for 12 months and was very beneficial.

2. CLOTHES

Men were provided with the following working clothes – shirt, shorts, gaiters, mining-cap, rubber and canvas shoes (*tabis*). A *bento*-box and cloth were provided for food. Replacements for worn out clothing became progressively harder to obtain, and for the last three months straw sandals (*warajis*) were the only footwear provided. For the first 12 months, there were no facilities for drying clothes for men working out-of-doors.

3. SABOTAGE

A commendable amount of quiet sabotage was maintained by all personnel. This included such activities as the continual and systematic removal of wedges, nuts, bolts, etc., from essential machinery. The most successful sabotage was at the shaft, where the Japanese ordered a special quick-drying cement mixture to be pumped down to stop the water. The British NCOs in charge altered the proportions to such an extent that the mixture was completely ineffective. This was never detected by the Japanese and, eventually, the whole project was abandoned because of flooding.

4. DANGERS

Only 4 out of some 150 men working in the mines had any previous experience. Many of the places in which men worked below were definitely dangerous.

The following table shows accidents sufficiently serious to cause hospitalisation or some permanent disability. In addition there were numerous accidents of a minor nature and frequent narrow escapes:

Major fractures	Incised	Contused	Factory
	0	0	0
Sanko Denki	0	1	0
Tateko	5	8	2
II Kofune	7	4	0
Kamoko	1	2	4
TOTALS	11	15	6

Killed at work: 2 men; 1 at Shaft; 1 at II Kofune

Fractured spine at work: 1 man at II Kofune.

Blinded in one eye at Kamoko: 1 man.

When accidents occurred, there was usually considerable delay in bringing the man to the surface, and, for anything less than a broken limb, a man often had to wait for the whole shift to finish and return to camp before medical attention could be received. No first-aid kit was kept underground. Some of the Japanese foremen took care to move men when danger was imminent, but a number were indifferent, so long as they themselves were not in the danger area. Some foremen were only 15 to 20 years old and were almost completely ignorant of mining work. For the first two months only, an official investigation followed all accidents at II Kofune.

5. TREATMENT

This varied entirely according to the individual Japanese foreman. A good foreman would be patient when making his requirements understood, would not hit the men, would give 40 mins interval for food and rest and would only expect a reasonable amount of work. A bad foreman would hit a man with fist or stick if he was not understood at once, would give 20 mins for rest and food, would stand over the men as they worked, shouting at them continuously, and would kick a man or hit him with whatever was handy, such as a pick, shovel, axe, stick, etc., if he stopped working for a moment. Foremen were roughly 20% good, 20% bad, and 60% varying between the two extremes, according to their feelings from day to day.

I made numerous applications to the various Japanese commandants to have all hitting of the men stopped. Results varied from approximately zero in the case of the first commandant to some beating up and suspension of foremen with the last – the latter change I consider to be probably due to the changing war position. The official attitude of the commandants to my complaints was that hitting of the men was not allowed, and they would 'take the matter up with the company'. Unofficially, it appeared that, so long as the foremen only used their hands or fists within moderation, they were reluctant to take action, but they would intervene when sticks or other weapons were used. Misunderstandings, due to the language difficulty, were undoubtedly the root cause of most troubles. No foreman could speak any English, although as time went on, in addition to 'speedo' 'stoppu' and 'O.K.' they began to bring out one or two rather unexpected expressions which will produce interesting reactions if aired as Kings English at some future date.

For the first 6 months, the Japanese drove the men really hard, but afterwards, although in theory the same amount of work was expected, in practice the majority of foremen developed a lack of interest in their country's war effort which became more and more marked, and the men took full advantage of this. If it had been otherwise, the combination of overwork and underfeeding would have killed many more men. Once a month 'prizes' were presented to 'good workers'. Such 'prizes' usually consisted of 20 cigarettes, plus a tablet of soap, or a couple of oranges, and were given to about 10% of the workers. For some two months, daily rewards of small bread rolls were presented to 'good workers'. The British distributed these on a roster system.

6. **PAY**

Pay was issued monthly at the following daily rates:

Warrant Officers: 25 sen
Sergeants & Corporals: 15 sen
Lance Corporals & Privates: 10 sen.

After 6 months these rates were increased by 5 yen per day.

7. CONCLUSION

Whether the mining done by the men in this camp was suitable for prisoners of war is one which I leave to experts on International Conventions. The Japanese will probably maintain that the conditions were the same for their own miners. I agree with this, but I hope that those who consider this plea will be thoroughly familiar with Japanese coal mines under war time conditions.

APPENDIX 7

Red Cross benefits received between 13.10.43 and 28.8.45

DATE	QUANTITY	DESCRIPTION
3.12.43	1 crate	Corned Beef
	2 x 100lb sacks	Sugar
	56lb	Cocoa
	5 crates	Tinned Meats
	32 individual parcels	

All above from the South African Red Cross

25.12.43	2 x 100lb sacks	Sugar
	28lb	Cocoa
26.1.44	5 crates	Canadian Red Cross
7.2.44	10 crates	Canadian Red Cross
16.2.44	10 crates	Canadian Red Cross
12.4.44	1 large carton	American Cigarettes
	1 large carton	Pipe tobacco
	60 Individual parcels	American Red Cross
29.4.44	60 individual parcels	American Red Cross
1.5.44	30 individual parcels	American Red Cross
21.5.44	60 individual parcels	American Red Cross
1.6.44	30 individual parcels	Canadian Red Cross
15.12.44	64 individual parcels	American Red Cross
1.1.45	96 individual parcels	American Red Cross
11.1.45	96 individual parcels	American Red Cross

DATE	QUANTITY	DESCRIPTION
21.1.45	96 individual parcels	American Red Cross
1.2.45	186 individual parcels	American Red Cross
15.2.45	94 individual parcels	American Red Cross
21.3.45	186 individual parcels	American Red Cross
17.5.45	380 individual parcels	American Red Cross
15.8.45	200 individual parcels	American Red Cross.

Other goods had been of meat, milk, fish, butter, jam, soap
only extracted before parcels arrived in Camp

CLOTHING (all from American Red Cross)

DATE	QUANTITY	DESCRIPTION
25.2.44	22 Bales	Assorted clothing
	30 Bales	Greatcoats
13.1.45	8 Bales	Assorted clothing
	60 Bales	Greatcoats

TOILET REQUISITES

DATE	QUANTITY	DESCRIPTION
Feb. 44	5 Cases	American Red Cross.
		Assorted toilet necessaries
Mar 45	5 Cases	As above

LEATHER BOOTS

DATE	QUANTITY	DESCRIPTION
During 1944	120 Pairs	American Red Cross

BOOKS

DATE	QUANTITY	DESCRIPTION
20.4.44	30 Volumes	(Also 20 copies of American Red Cross
3.3.45	50 Volumes	Newsletters: 4 copies for 5 different months – 1943/4)
23.4.45	200 Volumes	

MISCELLANEOUS

DATE	QUANTITY	DESCRIPTION
Feb. 1944	1 cobblers last,	Issued by Japanese as required, exact quantity soles, heels, nails, unknown) etc., for boot repairs

(**Author's note:** These cobbler's items were superfluous, as we had no boots to repair until the Red Cross consignment came later in 1944 – and those didn't wear out anyway, as the Japanese forbade us to wear them outside the camp!)

YMCA BENEFITS RECEIVED BETWEEN OCTOBER 1943 AND AUGUST 1944

100 Library Books (changed twice)

70 Pairs socks

50 Packs Playing cards

1 Guitar and spare strings

1 Mandolin and spare strings

1 Piano Accordion

5 Harmonicas

3 Footballs

MISCELLANEOUS BENEFITS

500 yen from Papal Delegate on occasion of his visit to camp.

1250 yen from American Red Cross to be divided amongst American PoWs in 11 Camp (2 Officers and 64 other ranks)

APPENDIX 8

Translation of speech by the Japanese Colonel
at No. 11 Camp, Fukuoka, on 20.8.45

I am pleased to inform you that we have received Military Orders for the stoppage of the war on the 18th August 1945.

Since you were interned in this camp, you have had, doubtlessly, to go through much trouble and agony due to the extension of your stay as prisoners of war. But you have overcome them and the news of the day for which you have longed day and night, the day on which you could return to your homeland where your beloved wives and children, parents, brothers and sisters are eagerly awaiting you, has become a fact, and probably your supreme joy. I would like to extend to you my most sincere congratulations, but at the same time I sympathise most deeply with those who have been unable due to illness or some other unfortunate reason, to greet this joyous day.

By order, we the camp staff have done all in our power towards your management and protection but owing to destitute internal conditions here, we regret that we are unable to do half of what we wanted to do for you but I trust in your great understanding on this point.

Several days ago at one camp, prisoners presented camp staff and factory foremen with part of their valuable foodstuffs and personal belongings, while at another camp, prisoners have asked for permission to present civilian war sufferers with their personal belongings. This, I know, is an expression of your understanding and your open-hearted gentlemanliness, and we, the camp staff, are deeply moved.

Until you are transferred to Allied hands at a port to be designated later, you will have to wait at this camp. Therefore I wish you will remain quietly for the day when you can return to your homeland, behaving according to regulations, holding fast your great honour as people of a Great Nation, and taking care of your health.

APPENDIX 9

Locations visited by the author from leaving the UK in 1941

By Sea

Left Gourock, Scotland on the *Warwick Castle* – December 1941
Arrived Freetown, West Africa – Christmas Day 1941
Cape Town, South Africa – Batavia, Java February 1941

Journey by road convoy: Batavia – Soerabaya
with 240 and 241 Batteries

Poelogadbone, Tjikarang; Krawang; Pananoekan; Djatibarang; Karangampel; Cheribon; Tegal; Pekalongan; Semarang; Salatiga; Bojolali; Soerakarta; Ngawi; Madion; Djombang; Madjokarta; Waroe; Soerabaya

Java – prior to capitulation

Tjelatap; Tasiikmalaja; Singapana; Garoet; Tjikajang; Tjisompet

Java – after capitulation

Tjibatoe; Bandoeng; Buitenzorg; Tandjong Priok; Cycle Camp; Boie Glodok; Tjimahi; Batavia

By Sea

Left Batavia for Singapore on the *Van Warwaek*

MISSING, BELIEVED KILLED

Changi Prison, Singapore

Left Singapore for Japan via Manila and Taiwan (Formosa) on the *Ussuri Maru*

Mainland Japan

Moji (Kyushu); Fukuoka (Camp 8); Nagasaki

Homeward Bound – September – November 1945

Nagasaki to Okinawa (U.S Destroyer *Cofer*)
Okinawa to Manila (Dakota DC-3 *Angel Ann* by air)
Manila to San Francisco via Pearl Harbour, Hawaii (*US Marine Shark*)
San Francisco to Oakland California (by ferry)

Oakland, California to Vancouver, Canada by US Railways via Eugene, Oregon; Portland, Oregon; Tacoma, Washington; and Seattle, Washington.

Vancouver, Canada to Toronto by Canadian Railways via Kamloops; Blue River; Wainwright; Saskatoon; Portage La Prairie; Sioux Lookout; Winnipeg; Foleyet and Capreol

Toronto to New Jersey via Syracuse, Albany and Weekhawken using the U.S Delaware & Hudson Railroad

New Jersey to New York (by ferry *Stony Point*)

New York to Southampton (by *S.S Queen Mary*) – November 1945

APPENDIX 10

Extract from document presented in evidence to the War Crimes Trials showing steps Japanese camp commandants were expected to take to rid themselves of PoWs

DOCUMENT No. 2701
(*Certified as Exhibit O in Doc No. 2687*)

From the Journal of the Taiwan PoW Camp HQ in Taihoku – entry made 1 August 1944

The following answer about the extreme measures for PoWs was sent to the Chief of Staff of the 11th Unit (Formosa PoW Security No. 10).

'Under the present situation if there were a mere explosion or fire, a shelter for the time being could be held in nearby buildings such as the school, warehouse, or the like. However, at such time as the situation became urgent and it be extremely important, the PoWs will be concentrated and confined in their present location and, under heavy guard; the preparation for the final disposition will be made.

The time and method of this disposition are as follows:

(1) THE TIME

Although the basic aim is to act under superior orders, **individual disposition** may be made in the following circumstances:

(a) When an uprising of large numbers cannot be suppressed without the use of firearms.

(b) When escapes from the camp may turn into a hostile fighting force.

(2) THE METHODS

(a) Whether they are destroyed individually or in groups, or however it is done, with mass bombing, poisonous smoke, poisons, drowning, decapitation, or what, dispose of them as the situation dictates.

(b) In any case it is the aim not to allow the escape of a single one, to annihilate them all, and not to leave any traces.

(3) TO: THE COMMANDING GENERAL
THE COMMANDING GENERAL
OF MILITARY POLICE

I hereby certify that this is a true translation from the

Journal of the Taiwan PoW HQ in Taiwan, entry 1
August 1944

Signed: Stephen H. Green

This is Exhibit marked 'O' referred to in the Affidavit
of JAMES THOMAS NEHEMIAH CROSS.

Sworn before me this 19th day of September 1946
Signed P.A.L. Vine, MAJOR R.M.